Sweet and Sour Pie

Sweet and Sour Pie

A Wisconsin Boyhood

Dave Crehore

Terrace Books
A trade imprint of the University of Wisconsin Press

Terrace Books
A trade imprint of the University of Wisconsin Press
1930 Monroe Street, 3rd Floor
Madison, Wisconsin 53711-2059

www.wisc.edu/wisconsinpress/

3 Henrietta Street
London WC2E 8LU, England

1   3   5   4   2

Printed in the United States of America

Library of Congress Cataloging-in-Publication Data
Crehore, Dave.
Sweet and sour pie : a Wisconsin boyhood / Dave Crehore.
    p.   cm.
ISBN 978-0-299-23060-9 (hardcover : alk. paper)
ISBN 978-0-299-23063-0 (e-book)
   1. Crehore, Dave—Childhood and youth.
   2. Manitowoc (Wis.)—Biography.
3. Manitowoc (Wis.)—Social life and customs.
                I. Title.
    F586.42.C74C74   2009
       977.5´67—dc22
            [B]
        2008039538

Disclaimer
In the interest of privacy, respect, and common sense,
many names of people and places that appear in this book have been changed,
and some characters and events are composites.

To
Mom and Dad,
and
small-town people everywhere.

Contents

Contents

Acknowledgments

Readers of this book will ask themselves how a kid managed to remember so much. The answer is that Mom and Dad did most of the remembering. My recollections of the fun and tribulation of our early years together—our Christmases and Thanksgivings, our hunting and fishing trips, and our lost dogs, along with so much else—are rooted in family tales that were told at the fireside or around the kitchen table, after Mom poured us a second cup of coffee and said, "Do you remember the time . . ."

So, thanks to you, Mom and Dad, for your memories and your willingness to share them. And thank you for not buying a television set until 1959. A home free of the tube gave the three of us time to read and dream, to talk and listen, to wander in the woods and learn the birds and the trees.

Further acknowledgements are due to a couple of corporations and a very important person.

First, thanks to the Eastman Kodak Company for manufacturing Kodachrome slide film. Some of the stories in this book were inspired and verified by slides Dad took in the forties and fifties, images that are as sharp and colorful today as they were back then. I wonder if digital pictures made today will be as useful, or even in existence, fifty or sixty years from now.

Second, thanks of a sort to the telephone companies of the fifties. Long-distance calls were expensive and time-consuming in those days, so we wrote letters to each other, letters that became lasting, written records of our lives. Few experiences are as bittersweet as discovering, in the papers of a deceased grandfather, a stack of one's childhood letters to him, carefully preserved and held together with a red rubber band.

Finally, voluminous thanks go to my wife, Joanne, for her support during the writing of this book. Many book acknowledgements contain that line—"thank you for your support"—without explaining it. In this case, support meant reading and re-reading, out loud, the many drafts of these stories, so that I could correct their sound. It also meant mowing the lawn, doing the dishes, and cleaning the house while I was engaged in the holy process of writing. So thanks again for your support, Jo. I can hardly wait to start another book.

Earlier versions of some of the stories in this book have been previously published.

"The Fine Art of Forgetting," "How Now, Frau Blau?" "The Dorking Rooster-Catcher," and "The Man of Action" were published in *Shooting Sportsman* magazine and in *Wisconsin Natural Resources* magazine.

"The Viggle Years," "The Digging Out of Nip," "The Century Run," "Sacrificing Sweet Sixteen," "The Secret Smallmouth Lake in the U.P.," "The Butternut Buck," "The Celebrated Water Witch of Door County," and "Sweet and Sour Pie" were published in *Wisconsin Natural Resources* magazine.

The remaining six stories, as well as "Envoi" and the "Glossary," appear here for the first time.

Sweet and Sour Pie

Beans for Breakfast

Let's find a church that looks like it's paid for," Dad said. "An old one without a mortgage."

Tuesday, August 15, 1950, was our second day in Manitowoc, Wisconsin. Mom, Dad, our beagle, Rip, and I were scouting the town in our Studebaker Champion; Dad drove while Mom paged through the phone book and plotted our position on a map. Our mission that morning was to locate a Methodist church, the A&P, and a store that sold bed frames.

I was seven and shared the back seat with Rip. As we cruised up one street and down another, Mom and Dad were having a good time, pointing out taverns with interesting names: the Stop and Go Inn, Leof's Spa, the Wonder Bar, the Foam Tavern, the Gay Bar, and the Tip Top Tap.

"Sure are a lot of them," Dad said.

Mom opened the Yellow Pages to "Taverns" and started to count, pursing her lips and running a pencil down the long list. "There are eighty-five, to be precise," she said. She flipped back to "Churches" and counted again. "And twenty-three churches."

"It's the eternal struggle," Dad said. Mom laughed, and I was surprised that she and Dad were in such high spirits, because the past twenty-four hours had been rough on them.

The movers had arrived the day before, a couple of hours after we did. The marine engineering company Dad worked for had transferred him to Manitowoc from Lorain, Ohio, a steel mill and shipyard city on Lake Erie. They had hired an outfit called Budget Boys to do the moving, and we soon found out how the Budget Boys got their name: they filled our house with boxes but didn't unpack them. As soon as the van was empty, the driver demanded Dad's signature on the moving contract and started the engine. When Dad protested, the driver pointed to some fine print, let in his clutch, and hit the road.

"Buncha cheapskates," Dad muttered, meaning the Budget Boys, his employer, or maybe both.

All we could do was go back in the house and start rummaging. In Ohio, Mom had labeled each box with its destination in Manitowoc—living room, kitchen, master bedroom, dining room. But the Budget Boys hadn't read Mom's labels, so practically every box and piece of furniture had to be moved again from one room to another. Luckily for us, in their rush to get going the Boys left a furniture dolly behind. We claimed it as a spoil of war and used it for years.

Dad started trundling boxes back and forth, upstairs and down. After an hour or so he called from upstairs.

"Charlotte, is our bed frame in the living room? It should be in a long narrow box. Look for Davy's, too."

Mom dug around in the maze of cartons and furniture. "I see the mattresses and springs, but no frames," she said. "Oh, for cripes sake," Dad said. "They must have left them in Lorain. We'll have to buy new ones tomorrow. Now I'm definitely going to keep this dolly."

It was getting dark and pretty cold for August. Dad and Mom lugged the mattresses upstairs. While Dad started a coal fire in the big furnace in the basement, Mom found a wool blanket and a war surplus GI sleeping bag, and we went to bed without supper. I spent the night in the sleeping bag and it was kind of fun, like camping indoors. Mom and Dad tried to cover themselves with the blanket, which was barely big enough for two.

Mom lay awake most of the night, shivering and staring at the ceiling. She finally dropped off about four in the morning, but when the first hint of dawn filtered into the bedroom, she woke up, turned on her side, and recoiled in horror.

A large bat was hanging on the wall about four feet away.

"Dammit, there's a bat!" she yelled. "Dave, wake up, there's a bat on the wall!" She pulled the blanket away from Dad and tried to hide under it.

Wrenched from a deep sleep, Dad rolled off the mattress and landed on his back. He staggered to his feet and hitched up the baggy undershorts he had slept in. Mom kept on complaining from under the blanket.

"All right, all right," Dad said. "I see it!"

"Good!" Mom said. "Now get rid of it!"

"OK," Dad said, shaking off the last of his sleep. "I'll figure out something, and in the meantime, Charlotte, be quiet. You'll just scare it."

"I don't care," Mom said. "It scared me first!"

The racket woke me up, and I walked down the hall from my

room to see what was going on. Rip, who had been sleeping on a corner of my bedroll, yawned and stretched and followed me. I took in the situation—the bat on the wall, Dad matching wits with it, Mom under the blanket—and came up with a solution that would be obvious to any seven-year-old boy.

"I know where the pistol is!" I said. I had watched the movers pack Dad's .22 Colt Woodsman and thought I could find the box it was in.

"No, no," Dad said. "We're not going to start shooting holes in the walls on our second day in Wisconsin. Besides, I don't know where the ammunition is."

Then his face brightened. "I've got it!" he said. He turned to me. "Hang on to Rip, stay right where you are, and don't make that bat fly," he said. "Just leave him alone."

Dad went downstairs, out the front door, and across the lawn to the garage, still barefoot and in his underwear. The movers had put our tools and camping gear in the garage, and in a couple of minutes Dad was back in the bedroom with an old-fashioned corn popper, a long-handled wire basket with a sliding metal lid.

"Charlotte, not a sound," he whispered, and began a stalk, tip-toeing across the bedroom. With a lightning thrust he clapped the corn popper over the bat and closed the lid, scraping the bat off the wall and into the basket.

"Aha!" Dad exulted. "Charlotte, you can come out now, I've got him!"

Mom's fingertips appeared, then an eye, an ear, and another eye. Dad poked the corn popper at her. The bat squeaked and flapped its wings. "See, he's in here," Dad said.

Mom pulled the blanket over herself again. "David Roger Cre-hore," she said through clenched teeth, "if you intend to keep on sleeping in this bedroom, you will remove that bat, right now!"

"You got it," Dad said, and went outside to let it go. Wrapped in the blanket, Mom walked warily down the hall to the bathroom, still on the lookout for bats. Before she closed the door, she looked at me and rolled her eyes. "Life in Wisconsin," she said.

We had a quick, cold breakfast. Mom hunted through boxes in the living room until she found some canned goods, silverware, her tea kettle, and a couple of ancient tea bags.

"We've got a choice," she said, looking over the cans. "Pork and beans or Ken-L Ration." Dad hacked open a can of each with his pocket knife, and we took turns dipping the beans out with teaspoons. The lone piece of pork was almost pure fat; we gave it to Rip along with the Ken-L Ration. When the kettle boiled, Dad rinsed out the bean can, put in a tea bag, poured hot water over it, and handed the can to Mom.

"Would Madam care for a can of tea?" he asked.

"Thank you, Jeeves," Mom said. She waited a few minutes for it to steep and took a sip. The surface of the tea had an oil slick from the pork.

"Ahh," she sighed. "Gracious living in Manitowoc." Then we hit the road.

As it turned out, there were two Methodist churches in Manitowoc, Saint Paul's on North Seventh and Wesley on the south side. Saint Paul's was a frame building that had probably been paid for in the 1880s. Wesley looked a lot newer. "I vote for Saint Paul's," Dad said, and the decision was made.

The A&P wasn't hard to find, down Eighth Street, Manitowoc's main drag, and a few blocks west on Washington. We bought a loaf of Ann Page bread, a pound of butter, some Eight O'Clock coffee, hamburger, onions, celery, cans of kidney beans and stewed tomatoes, and a tin of cayenne pepper. "If I can find the dutch oven," Mom said, "I'll make a batch of chili to get us through the next couple of days."

We bought new bed frames at Otto Kuechle's, a furniture store at Ninth and Jay. Once Mom and Dad had picked out frames that would fit our mattresses and springs, the salesman folded his arms across his chest, the embodiment of rock-solid integrity.

"I stand behind all the beds I sell," he said.

"That won't be necessary," Dad said. "But I could use some help getting 'em in the car."

The Studie was parked outside Kuechle's front door, and a small crowd of helpful spectators gathered on the sidewalk as Dad and the salesman rolled down the windows and tried various approaches. The spectators offered suggestions. One guy got a toolbox from the trunk of his car and offered to take the frames apart; another volunteered the use of his pickup truck.

Finally Dad decided to stow the frames transversely across the backseat, with the bedposts sticking out of the windows like the cannons on "Old Ironsides." When we were ready to go the spectators introduced themselves and petted Rip. There were handshakes all around, and as we drove off, they waved.

"Nice people," Dad said. "Small-town people."

On our way back to the house Dad bought a dollar's worth of gas—3.7 gallons—at the Sinclair station on North Eleventh, and we stopped for sundaes at the Park Drug Store on New York Avenue. In the 1950s, if you wanted a sundae you went to the soda fountain at a drugstore.

"You folks new around here?" the pharmacist asked, as he scooped dishes of vanilla and pumped chocolate syrup over them. It was a small store and the pharmacist doubled as manager and soda jerk.

"We're just moving in," Dad said. "Out River Road, up the hill and to the right."

"Oh, you mean the old Torrison place," the pharmacist said.

When we finished our sundaes we headed west. "The old Torrison place, eh? Seems like our house has a pedigree," Dad said. "I wonder when they'll start calling it the old Crehore place."

"Never, if I see another bat," Mom said. She liked to fish and didn't mind baiting her own hook, but she drew the line at bats.

We spent the rest of the day unpacking. That night Dad built a fire in the living room fireplace to drive out any bats that might be lurking in the flue. When the fire was burning nicely he popped some corn over it and took a bowl into the kitchen where Mom was sitting at the table, reading through the *Manitowoc Herald-Times*. The front page was full of gloomy news about the Korean War and an earthquake, but there were a few bright spots inside.

"Kroger's has chuck roast for $0.69 a pound," Mom said, "and Penney's is selling dress shirts with nonwilting collars for $1.75. And how about this—the Studebaker dealer has a Champion just like ours for $1,517.63, brand new and delivered."

"Too much," Dad said. "We only paid $1,450.00 in Lorain."

Mom put a handful of popcorn in her mouth and continued to read. "Needs more salt," she said. Suddenly she looked up from the paper and stopped chewing.

"How did you make this?" she asked.

"In the wire popper," Dad said. Mom blew a shower of half-chewed kernels onto the table.

"A bat was in there!" she said. She went to the sink, ran a glass of water, and rinsed out her mouth.

"Charlotte, I was holding the popper over an open fire. It's sterilized."

"I don't care!" Mom said. "That popcorn has bat stuff in it. Give it to Rip."

"The last thing we need in the house is a dog full of popcorn," Dad said. "I'll eat it."

"Don't expect a good-night kiss," Mom said.

"All right, all right," Dad said. "I'll give it to the chipmunks." He headed for the back door with the bowl. "Not exactly a daughter of the pioneers, are you?" he said.

"You got it," Mom said.

In fact, back in northern Ohio, Mom's ancestors had been pioneers. But 150 years had gone by since then, and most of our Ohio relatives were city people who had never been west of Toledo. In their minds, "Manitowoc, Wisconsin" called up sinister images of brooding forests and drooling wolves. They suspected that Dad's transfer had sentenced Mom to a short and nasty life in the woods. "Poor Charlotte," they whispered, as they shot glances at her and tut-tutted sympathetically.

But Manitowoc was no wilderness. In 1950 we found it to be Germanic, *gemütlich* and obsessively neat, a shipbuilding and manufacturing town of about twenty-seven thousand bounded by Lake Michigan on the east, farms on the west and south, and the small city of Two Rivers to the north.

Our house was a former hunting lodge on River Road, just outside the western city limits and on the edge of a deep, wooded ravine that was the forest primeval to me. Across the road was a dairy farm with craggy Holstein cows and bulls. They bellowed at all hours, made green muffins the size of manhole covers, and occasionally rode each other.

"Circus cows," I called them, until Dad explained what they were doing. In those days bulls and cows carried out their romances in plain sight, without technical assistance and purely for the fun of it. I felt pretty grown up after I understood what was going on, and appreciated Manitowoc a lot more. One thing Lorain didn't have was cows in love.

But a certain break-in period was required before we got used to

Manitowoc and it got used to us. For openers there was our struggle with Clem Becker, Wisconsin Bell, and Augie from Whitelaw.

Clem Becker was a wholesale meat dealer in Two Rivers. Farmers with cows to sell called him early in the morning to check prices. But as soon as our phone was hooked up we started getting calls to Clem from a farmer named Augie who lived in the crossroads village of Whitelaw, a couple of miles west of us. The first day after the phone was installed, it rang about 5:00 a.m. and Dad ran downstairs to answer it.

"Hey, Clem?" the caller said. "This is Augie."

In the background Dad could hear the clang of milk pails and a chorus of moos.

"You've got the wrong number," Dad responded. "This is Dave Crehore in Manitowoc."

But the farmer couldn't hear Dad over the noise in the barn.

"Whatcha payin' for canners and cutters today, Clem?" Augie asked. "I got a load ready to go."

"I'm not paying anything," Dad said. "I'm not in the cattle business."

"What did you say?" the farmer asked. "You're not in business? Chrissake, Clem, what happened?"

Dad gently hung up the phone, went into the kitchen, lit his pipe, and put the coffee on. Just about the time the percolator began to gurgle, the phone rang again.

"Hey, Clem? Augie!"

"This isn't Clem. You've got the wrong number again. This is 2-3515 in Manitowoc. If you want to talk to Clem, call his number."

"I am calling his number," the farmer said. "Been calling it for years. I got it written right here on the milkhouse wall. It's 2-3515 in Two Rivers!"

"That's my number too," Dad said, "but 2-3515 in Manitowoc."

"Well, that's a helluva note," Augie said. "I'll call Clem and get it straightened out."

"No, don't call Clem, you'll just get me again!"

"I suppose so," Augie said. "Hey, it was nice talking to you, anyway. I gotta finish milking. Good-byc!"

"Yeah, good-bye."

Dad figured Augie's calls were just a one-time comedy of errors until the same thing happened the next morning. Then he called the phone company and got a supervisor. The supervisor seemed to think Dad was pulling her leg.

"You're telling me that calls from Whitelaw to a butcher in Two Rivers are going to you in Manitowoc?" she asked.

"So it would appear," Dad said. "Some of them, anyway. We've got the same number, and your equipment can't tell the difference."

"Mr. Crehore, that is impossible."

"Tell you what," Dad said. "You be here about five o'clock tomorrow morning and find out just how possible it is."

"Now, let's not lose our tempers . . ."

During September, we heard from Augie once or twice a week. He always apologized and made some small talk before getting back to his milking. In October and November his calls dwindled to one a month, and we got what turned out to be his last call in late December.

"Hey, Clem?"

"Nope, you've got Dave again."

"Jesus Christ, I'm sorry."

"It's OK, Augie, I'm an early riser anyway. Merry Christmas!"

"Hey, Merry Christmas, Dave." Augie said. "Good-bye—I gotta finish the milking."

We never heard from him again; either the phone company had solved the problem or Augie had sold his cows. We kind of missed him for a while.

There was some trouble with the mail, too. Our Ohio friends and relatives could spell Crehore, of course, but they had a lot of trouble with Manitowoc. And our new Wisconsin friends could spell Manitowoc but insisted on translating Crehore, which is Irish, into various German equivalents. In early January of 1951, we got a blizzard of Christmas cards forwarded to us from various Creagers, Cramers, and Crugers, and from places like Manawa, Manistee, and Manistique. Mail from people who couldn't spell Crehore or Manitowoc wasn't a problem, since it never got to us.

Finally, there were difficulties with the spoken language. Among other things, we faced the pop/soda confusion and the mystery of "enso."

A few days after we moved in, Dad drove to Felix Woytal's Clover Farm Store in the nearby hamlet of Manitowoc Rapids to pick up some groceries. Rip loved to ride in the car, so Dad took him along.

Among Dad's purchases was a six-pack of Coca-Cola, which in those days cost about a quarter and came in eight-ounce glass bottles. Felix punched the price of each item into the register and hit the total bar. The cash drawer jumped out and Felix made change. "Two forty-nine, two fifty, three, four, five," he said, as he dropped the coins and singles into Dad's hand. Then he began bagging the cans and boxes. When he got to the Coke, he paused.

"You want the soda in a bag?" he asked.

Dad looked at his shopping list. As far as he knew, soda was a white powder that came in an orange box with an arm and hammer on it. Every now and then Mom asked him to buy some. But he was sure he hadn't bought any that day.

"I don't believe I had any soda," Dad said.

"Well, here it is, right here," Felix said, and picked up the Coke.

"Oh," Dad said. "See, where I come from we call that 'pop.'"

Felix narrowed his eyes and gave Dad a once-over. "Pop?" he said, doubtfully. "Where do you come from?" he asked.

"Up the hill and a half-mile east on River Road," Dad said.

"I mean before that," Felix said.

"We just moved here from Ohio."

"Ohio," Felix said, as though that explained a lot. He smiled and pushed the bags of groceries toward Dad. "That's the one that's round on the ends and high in the middle, enso?"

Dad smiled back, but he couldn't laugh at Felix's joke, which was old even in 1950.

Felix didn't mind. "Well, it's a nice day, enso?" he said.

That made two "ensos," thrown in for no apparent reason. Dad had understood Felix to say "and so . . ." and waited for him to finish his sentence.

There was a short silence. To hurry things along, Dad asked, "And so . . . what?"

"And so nothing, just enso," Felix said. Exasperation was creeping into his voice. Dad picked up his groceries and left.

Outside, he found the windows of the Studebaker fogged with beagle breath and smeared with nose prints. Rip was jumping from the backseat to the front and back again, barking and keeping an eye on two scruffy terriers that were peeing on the Studie's tires.

"Beat it!" Dad said. "Enso, or whatever the magic word is. Scram!"

The terriers ran to a bucket by the side of the store to tank up on water, and then came back and flopped down in the shade of the gas pumps to sleep until the next car pulled up. Dad bent down and fondled their ears while they smiled and panted at him.

It occurred to Dad that having your tires peed on by gas pump dogs was part of the small-town life he was learning to lead, and he kind of liked it. "Such a deal, boys," Dad said to the terriers. "Nothing to do but drink, eat, sleep, bark, and piss. A lot of people would trade places with you in a minute."

A few days later, a neighbor translated "enso" for us.

"My wife spoke German at home," he said, "and she says 'enso' comes from *nicht wahr?* which is German for 'not true?' When Germans talk to other Germans, they stick *nicht wahr?* on the end of every other sentence to be polite. So in English it probably started out as 'ain't it so?' and finally got worn down to 'enso.'"

Once we knew what it meant, we were tempted to say "enso" just like the natives, but we never really got the hang of it.

While we were moving in, one of the first things Mom unpacked was her Sears and Roebuck Silvertone radio. When Dad was gone during the war she had left it on all day, just for company, and got hooked on soap operas like *Ma Perkins, The Romance of Helen Trent, Just Plain Bill, Our Gal Sunday, Portia Faces Life,* and *Young Dr. Malone.* She usually followed six soaps at a time, somehow keeping track of the characters' tangled lives and endless disappointments.

Dad preferred the evening comedy shows like *Duffy's Tavern* and *Fibber McGee and Molly* and comedians like Fred Allen, Jack Benny, and Red Skelton. But he admired Mom's ability to keep up with the flimsy plots of her soaps. "It beats me, Charlotte," he used to say, "how you can remember all those stories at once."

"It comes from having a degree in English literature," Mom said. "If you can follow Jane Austen, you can follow Helen Trent."

One afternoon during our first week in Manitowoc, Mom was trying to tune in *Ma Perkins* and got classical music instead. She listened for a while and learned the source: WOMT, the voice of Manitowoc, at 1240 on the AM dial.

If Ma wasn't available a little culture wouldn't hurt, Mom figured, so she left the music on while she was getting supper ready. The announcer was a local man who had a good radio voice but was more at home with polkas.

"And-a now," he intoned, "that wartime favorite, the symphony number five by Ludwig van Beethoven, played for your listening pleasure by Arthur Toscanini and his orchestra."

He cued up the first 78-rpm record and started the thirty-minute symphony with only fifteen minutes left in the show. Mom gritted her teeth when he faded out of the andante con moto and into a commercial for Dick Brothers Bakery. But after a while she got used to it. Beethoven with commercials was better than no Beethoven at all.

School started right after Labor Day. Because we lived outside the city limits, I had to go to the State Graded School in Manitowoc Rapids, about a mile and a half away. It was a two-story yellow brick building with an aroma of fuel oil, floor wax, old sneakers, and chalk. There were three classrooms: kindergarten through second grade; third grade through fifth, taught by Mrs. Eberhardt; and upstairs, grades six through eight, taught by Mr. Lensmire. I do not mention their first names because in those days teachers were called Miss, Missus, or Mister. As far as kids were concerned, teachers did not have first names.

My first day at Rapids State Graded was a triumph. When I got there in the morning I was nominally a second-grader. Mr. Lensmire, the principal, looked over my school records from Lorain and handed me a copy of *The Poky Little Puppy*.

"Can you read this?" he asked. Could I read it! *The Poky Little Puppy* was a particular favorite of mine.

I began the first page of gentle, flowing prose. "Five little puppies dug a hole under the fence and went for a walk in the wide, wide world."

I turned the page. "Through the meadow they went, down the road, over the bridge, across the green grass, and up the hill, one after the other . . ."

"Very good," Mr. Lensmire said. He took some change from his pocket and put a half dollar, a quarter, a dime, a nickel, and three pennies on his desk. "How much is this?" he asked.

"Ninety-three cents," I said. He removed the quarter. "Sixty-eight." He removed the dime and one of the pennies. "Fifty-seven."

"Excellent," said Mr. Lensmire. "Two more questions. Do you know your phone number?"

"Yes, 2-3515."

"And when were you born?"

"November 17, 1942."

"You belong in third grade," he said. He took me by the hand and we walked down the stairs to Mrs. Eberhardt's room.

That morning, Mom had driven Dad to work at the shipyard and then dropped me off at school. Before she left, she asked a boy in the playground when the school day was over.

"The little kids get out at three and the big kids at three thirty," he said. Mom figured I was a little kid, so she came back at three, but not in the Studebaker. In the meantime her father, my Grandpa Lester, had arrived from Lorain on a visit. He was a tall, austere man who wore dark suits and drove a Packard Clipper, a bulbous bathtub of a car that competed unsuccessfully with Cadillac.

When I got outside, kids were standing around, admiring the Packard. I climbed into the backseat and the kids murmured.

"Where have you been?" Mom asked. "We've been waiting since three o'clock."

"Oh, don't you know?" I said proudly. "I'm in third grade now, and the big kids don't get out 'til three thirty." Grandpa began to snort, which was how he laughed.

"Get back in there," he said. "In a week you'll be all done!"

The next morning Grandpa drove me to school in the Packard. Kids were waiting for us to arrive.

"Jeez, kid, is that your show-fer?" one of them asked. "No, that's my grandpa," I said. They seemed relieved, but a grandpa with a Packard still made me a rich kid by Rapids standards. The Packard was a barrier between us.

Our relations were cordial but distant for a couple of days. Then Dad drove up one afternoon behind the wheel of a 1925 Model A Ford he had bought for fifty dollars as a go-to-work car. He was wearing greasy coveralls and a hard hat, and from then on I was one of the gang. Rapids kids understood old cars and coveralls and hard hats.

There were about thirty of us in Mrs. Eberhardt's room, ten or eleven in each grade, and it was a good system. When third grade was being taught, I had the advantage of individual attention, and when the fourth- or fifth-graders were reciting I could do my homework, look at green and purple countries on the big pull-down maps of the world, read library books, or listen in to get a head start on what I would learn the next year.

Rapids State Graded School didn't have a gym, so instead of physical education we had recess. Weather permitting, we spent recess improving our hand-eye coordination, the girls with a ball and jacks and the boys playing mumblety-peg with their pocketknives. Almost every Rapids boy started carrying a pocketknife when he was seven or eight; it was part of his basic equipment:

> Left front pocket: Knife
> Right front pocket: Pennies to buy candy at Felix
>   Woytal's store
> Left rear pocket: Handkerchief
> Right rear pocket: Billfold with a picture of Ava
>   Gardner but no bills
> Shirt pocket: Trading stock of baseball cards

We traded baseball cards because in 1950 the sixteen major league baseball teams ruled the world of professional sports; pro football and hockey were curiosities that showed up from time to time on the back page of the sports section. As a result, one of the high points of the Rapids State Graded year was our annual softball World Series, played during lunch hours in early October. We formed two teams with about twenty kids on a side, ranging in age from seven to fourteen. The teams were named after the pennant winners who were in the major league series each year, and in 1950, they were the Yankees and the Phillies. As a born Cleveland Indians fan I would have nothing to do with the Yankees, so I was a Philly.

It was difficult to fit twenty defensive players on our ball field in the vacant lot east of the school, but we managed it. There were two catchers, one behind the other, to cut down on passed balls. And in addition to the usual five infielders we put a "short fielder" in each gap, making the hit-and-run game pretty difficult to execute. The remaining eleven kids played outfield.

The field had a healthy stand of weeds, worn down to the bare dirt on the base paths. There was a rudimentary wire backstop behind home plate, but no outfield fence; instead there was a ditch that ran from the left to right field foul lines. The ditch was three or four feet deep and full of slimy green algae fertilized by the overflow from failing septic tanks.

A ball hit into the ditch was called a "sewie ball" and was scored as a ground rule double. A ball hit over the ditch was a home run, although no one had ever done it. To field a sewie ball, you scrambled down the side of the ditch, fished out the floating softball with the webbing of your glove and flipped the ball up onto the grass. Then you would kick it around for a while until it was reasonably dry and throw it in.

In the seventh and deciding game of our 1950 Rapids series, the Phillies led by one run in the bottom of the ninth, and the Yankees were at bat with the bases empty and two out. The Phillies needed one more out to win, and the tension grew as a fifth-grade girl named Vivian walked to the plate for the Yankees. She batted cross-handed and had never been known to hit a ball out of the infield. But this time she whacked a dribbler to left that dodged all the fielders and went into the ditch.

Mr. Lensmire was the umpire. "Sewie ball!" he shouted. "Vivian, take second."

I was playing deep left field and had to retrieve the ball. I tossed it to the pitcher. There had been four or five sewie balls in the last two innings, and it was getting waterlogged.

The game was at its crucial moment. With two out and Vivian in scoring position, a single or another sewie ball could tie it up. And given the uneven quality of our outfielders, some of whom did not have gloves, a long line drive could score two.

"Who's up?" I asked Doug Goeters, the fielder to my left. "Doyle," he said. "Oh, God," I said.

Doyle was the pride of the Yankees that year, a strapping eighth-grader who was big for his age and usually needed a shave. The infield chatter fell silent when he came to bat. He took a couple of savage warm-up swings and then glared at our pitcher, a sixth-grade girl named Ruthie.

"OK, ya little twerp, I dare ya," he growled. "Go ahead, strike me out!"

Ruthie challenged him with a perfect strike across the heart of the plate. There was a crack of bat on ball and a spray of sewage. We stood frozen in our tracks as we watched a towering fly soar to deep center. The nearest five or six outfielders overcame their awe and broke for the ball, but they didn't have a chance. Doyle's shot landed a good ten feet on the far side of the ditch, and the game ended with a walk-off two-run homer. The Rapids Yankees won, 27–26. The New York Yankees won that year too, drubbing the Phillies in four straight games.

The autumn wore on. The trees changed color, and before long there was a crackling frost every morning. The ground froze too hard to play mumblety-peg at recess. After Thanksgiving it seemed to snow every day. The gravel street that ran along the south side of the school grounds was too steep for cars to climb in the winter and it became our sledding hill. Kids who had sleds brought them to school and coasted down the hill at recess and lunch hour. At the end of each school day we stood our sleds up against the wall of the school and left them there overnight. No one ever bothered them.

Along with the snow, winter paid another dividend: government surplus food for lunch. There was a big gas range in the basement of the school, and early in the morning the teachers would begin baking and roasting. A couple of days a week we had huge baked potatoes swimming in surplus butter. And before Thanksgiving and Christmas there was turkey: big brown drumsticks and steaming slabs of white meat. No one ever told us why we got the surplus food, but I suppose it was because somebody in Washington thought we were poor.

At Christmas, Mom, Dad, and I drove down to Lorain to spend the holiday with Grandpa and Grandma Lester. We headed back to Manitowoc a couple of days later. Dad backed down Grandpa's driveway and waited for an opening in the traffic. Then he pulled out and shifted into low.

"And away we go," he said, "homeward bound." Mom looked at him.

"Do you realize what you just said?" she asked. "You called Manitowoc home."

"Isn't it?" Dad asked.

Mom hesitated for a minute. "Well, come to think of it, I guess it is," she said. "Enso?"

The Fannie Farmer Mystery

When you buy an old house on the outskirts of town, there's a good chance that some resident wildlife will be there to welcome you. At least, that was our experience.

A couple of days after we moved into our place on River Road, Mom was cleaning the kitchen drawers before stowing away the silverware and utensils.

"The people who lived here must have liked rye bread," she said. "These drawers are just full of caraway seeds."

Dad was in the dining room, washing the windows with vinegar water and an old T-shirt. He came into the kitchen to have a look.

"See for yourself," Mom said.

Dad opened a drawer and wiped it out with the T-shirt. "Charlotte, I hate to tell you this," he said, "but these little things aren't caraway seeds—they're mouse poop."

"Oh my God," Mom gasped. "Now what do we do?"

"Catch 'em, I guess," Dad said. "When I'm done with these windows I'll run in to the A&P and get some mousetraps. We should be able to thin them out in a week or so."

"All right," Mom agreed, "but don't go to the A&P. If you buy mousetraps there, they'll know we have mice."

"Charlotte, the A&P doesn't care if we have mice," Dad said.

"Yes, they do," Mom responded. "We were there the day before yesterday, and I don't want them whispering about us the next time we go in."

Dad sighed and shrugged his shoulders. "OK, OK, I'll go to the hardware store." He grinned at me and dug the car keys out of his pocket.

While Dad was gone Mom wiped out the drawers with bleach. "When you live in an old barn out in the sticks, you're going to be infested with things, I suppose," she said. "First there were bats in the bedroom, and now mice. What's next, rattlesnakes?"

"Mom, there was only one bat," I pointed out. I loved the house and wanted to defend it.

"Hah!" Mom said. "Where there's one, there's more. You wait and see."

Dad was back in about an hour. He had bought six mousetraps, two extra blades for his coping saw, a rat-tail file, a pound of eight-penny nails, and a set of screwdrivers. He was not to be trusted in hardware stores.

After Mom and I went to bed that night, Dad baited the traps with peanut butter, put them in the drawers, shut off the kitchen lights, and retired quietly to the dining room to await results. To pass the time he smoked his pipe and worked on the newspaper crossword. It took him about ten minutes to fill in as many of the horizontal words as he could, and he had just started on the verticals when there was a loud snap in the kitchen. Satisfied, he went to bed, setting his alarm clock for five-thirty. He wanted to be up early to run his trapline.

But the shipyard beat him to the punch. At ten after five the phone rang and he ran downstairs to answer it. Someone at the yard wanted him to drive in and witness a hydrostatic test, right away.

"I'll be there in fifteen minutes," Dad said, and hung up. He put on a pair of white coveralls, rubber boots, and a tin hat. "I'll be home for lunch," he hollered.

"Fine," Mom said.

I got up at about seven o'clock and went downstairs to see what was for breakfast. Mom was sitting at the kitchen table, drinking coffee and staring grimly out the window.

"Don't even look in the drawers," she said. "They're full of dead mice." She rummaged in the refrigerator and pulled out a quart of milk, a loaf of bread, a stick of butter, and a jar of apricot jam. "I guess it will be safe to have toast," she said. "I don't think our little friends have invaded the icebox or the toaster."

When I had finished my toast I whistled up Rip, and the two of us went outside to explore the woods across the road. It seemed like a good morning to stay out of the house.

Dad came home for lunch at about noon and found Mom still sitting at the table. "I haven't been able to get a single thing done this morning," she complained. "I can't turn around without finding another dead mouse. Please empty those traps."

Dad opened the drawers and dropped the mousetraps in an old grocery bag. He had caught six mice, which he threw into the garbage can on the back porch.

"Charlotte, it's not like they're rats or anything," he said. "They're actually kind of attractive."

Mom turned away and dabbed at her eyes with a corner of her apron.

24

"That's just it," she said, her voice fluttering. "They're such dear little things. I don't want them running around the house, but I can't stand seeing them in those traps, either. I just don't know what to do!"

She looked up at Dad and tried to smile. Dad smiled back. Any woman who felt sorry for mice was his kind of girl.

"Well, just hang in there for the moment," he said. "I'll think of something." He put his arm around her shoulders. "By the way, what's for lunch?"

"Nothing much," Mom said. "I suppose I could make you a peanut butter sandwich." Dad winced.

"No, thanks—peanut butter doesn't appeal to me right now," he said. "I'll get a hamburger someplace."

Mid-afternoon found Dad sitting at his desk at the shipyard, planning the eviction of unwanted animals from his house. He was wondering what to do about the large and furry spiders he had found lurking in the coal bin when something brushed against his leg.

"Gaah!" he shouted, and stood up so suddenly he tipped over his swivel chair. A long-haired black cat the size of a lynx came out from under his desk and rubbed itself against his ankle. "Merr-row," it said.

Dad walked down the hall to the next office. The cat kept pace with him like a dog at heel. He cleared his throat to attract the attention of the man in the office, who was doing something complicated with a slide rule and a ten-row calculator.

"Hey, Ernie, who owns this cat?"

"You mean Fritz?" the man replied. "He's kind of community property. He's been around here about a year. The janitor fixed up a box and a bed for him in the basement, and we feed him scraps from our lunches."

"Do you think anybody would mind if I borrowed him for a couple of days?" Dad asked. "I have some mice to get rid of."

"Be my guest," Ernie responded. "He's not only the biggest cat in Manitowoc, he's also the best mouser. This building was overrun with mice when he showed up, but you hardly ever see one now."

Dad went back to his office, with Fritz by his side. He picked up his fallen chair, sat down, and stroked Fritz, who began to purr with a visceral vibration that reminded Dad of a Scott-Atwater outboard motor. He wasn't particularly fond of cats, but he didn't question fate, which had presented him with a friendly, mobile mousetrap just when he needed one.

When Dad got home from work later that afternoon he was carrying Fritz in a cardboard box. He set the box on the floor inside the front door and called a family council.

"Charlotte, Davy, I think I've solved the mouse problem. Come in here and bring Rip." He explained to us about Fritz and let Rip sniff the box. Rip was normally a placid dog, but at the first scent of cat he bristled as though his tail had been plugged into a socket.

"Oh, great," Dad said. "I was afraid of that. Davy, hold on to Rip's collar. I'm going to show him the cat."

Dad reached into the box, took Fritz by the scruff of the neck, lifted him up, and held him securely with both arms. "See the nice kitty, Rip?" he said. There was a moment of silence while Rip and Fritz looked at each other. I held Rip's collar with both hands while he sized up the situation.

"Let him go, Davy," Dad commanded, and we all held our breaths.

Rip was pretty smart for a beagle. He took another long look at Fritz, dropped his tail, and retreated to the back hall.

Dad put Fritz on the living room floor, not knowing whether he would hide under the couch or chase after Rip. But Fritz did neither; instead, he ambled amiably around the house, getting the lay of the land. When Rip came into the kitchen, Fritz calmly moved into the dining room, and when Fritz returned to the kitchen, Rip side-stepped him and went into the den. As we watched, the animals worked out ways to stay away from each other. There was no spitting, growling, clawing, or curtain climbing.

"I wish the Republicans could see this," Dad said.

At bedtime Dad shut Rip in my room and called Fritz into the kitchen. He opened all the drawers and cabinets, and showed Fritz the door to the cellar stairs. "There you go," Dad said. "Good luck and good hunting."

The following morning the shipyard called early again. When Dad went downstairs to answer the phone he found a present from Fritz on the antique marble-topped table we used for a telephone stand: five dead mice laid out like corpses on a slab. The next morning there were three mice on the telephone stand, then one, and then none. After supper on Fritz's fifth day with us, Dad slid his chair back from the table and lit his pipe.

"Let's see," he said. "I caught six mice in the mousetraps, Fritz's total so far is nine, and we haven't found any fresh caraway seeds in the kitchen. I suppose I can take Fritz back to the office tomorrow."

"Do you have to?" Mom asked. "I'd like to keep him here another week, just to be on the safe side." But Fritz's visit was cut short by an incident that went down in the family annals as the Fannie Farmer mystery.

As a rule, Dad gave Mom four boxes of candy a year: for her birthday in December, on their anniversary in February, for Mother's Day, and in August or September, just on general principles. Usually he bought Whitman's Samplers, but that night he had brought home a rare extravagance, a triple-decker box of five dozen assorted Fannie Farmer candies, including chocolates, pecan pralines, and Jordan almonds.

The Depression and wartime rationing had taught Mom to

conserve, and when she got her boxes of candy she hid them and dispensed the pieces like medicine, one per person every other day or so. The morning after the candy arrived I asked Mom for a piece, but as usual the answer was no.

"We'll have some after supper tomorrow," she said. Candy always came tomorrow, never today. I decided to take matters into my own hands.

Later that morning, while Mom was doing the laundry in the basement, I found the Fannie Farmer box tucked away in her closet. With infinite care, I dug down to the bottom layer, removed a handful of chocolates, replaced the cardboard dividers, and put the lid back on. At the rate Mom handed out candy, I figured, she wouldn't get down to the bottom of the box until well into September, and that was too far off to worry about.

That afternoon, Rip and I were building a dam across the creek that ran through our ravine when I heard Mom calling me from the back porch.

"David Henry Crehore," she yelled, "come here this instant!" The use of my full name meant I was in trouble; Mom must have discovered that I had raided her candy, but I couldn't imagine how.

When I got to the house Mom was in the kitchen waiting for me, her arms folded across her ribs. The box of candy was on the table. Somehow, she had found me out.

"Shame on you, you greedy thing!" she said. "There were sixty pieces of candy in this box to begin with. We each had a piece last night, so there should be fifty-seven left, but I just counted and there are only fifty-three."

"Someone," she continued, giving me a case-hardened look, "has taken four pieces of candy without permission, and it wasn't me."

No one can be as outraged and offended as a small boy who has been found guilty on circumstantial evidence. I folded my arms in duplication of Mom's pose. "Well, it wasn't me either!" I lied. "I didn't even know where the damn candy was!"

"You watch your mouth," Mom said. "Just wait until your father gets home!"

Turning on my heel, I stamped down the back hall and slammed the door behind me. I crossed the yard in big strides and went back into the ravine to sulk. Rip trotted along with me, and when we were out of sight of the house I sat on the ground and gathered him into my arms. He licked my face while I sniffled and muttered dire threats. "It's not fair!" I said to Rip. "No one but my mother would actually count candy. What's the matter, doesn't she trust me?"

After a while I calmed down and finished building my dam. A pool was forming behind it when I heard Mom calling me again. *What the hell does she want now?* I wondered, as I climbed the side of the ravine.

When I reached the yard, Mom came running and enveloped me in a smothering hug. "I'm sorry, I'm sorry, Davy," she said. "It wasn't you who took the candy."

I looked up at her. "Who was it?" I asked.

"Well, you'll never believe it . . . ," Mom said. At that moment Dad chugged up the driveway in the Studebaker. He got out of the car and walked over to us. "What's going on?" he asked. Mom released me from the hug.

"Mice or no mice, Fritz has got to go back to the shipyard!" she said. "Come inside and I'll tell you about it."

Dad and I sat at the kitchen table while Mom dumped ground coffee in our big enamelware percolator and put it on the stove.

"It's like this," she began. "I put the box of candy on the bottom shelf in my bedroom closet last night, and about two o'clock this afternoon I thought I'd have one of those raspberry bonbons. I opened the box and found that there were four pieces missing."

She reached across the table and took my hand in a warm grip. "I blamed Davy and gave him Hail Columbia," she said, "but a little later I decided to put the candy somewhere else. I went back up to my closet, and you'll never guess what I found."

"One of the neighbors," Dad said.

"No, no, no," Mom said, laughing. "It was a chipmunk. The cutest little chipmunk, sitting up on his haunches and eating a Jordan almond. He was holding it in his little hands and licking the sugar."

"But I forgot that Fritz was with me—you know how he follows me around—and when he saw the chipmunk he went for it. For a minute there were animals everywhere, and then the chipmunk went under my shoe rack and just disappeared. I found a little hole in the paneling behind the shoe rack, so that must be how he got in and out."

"Anyway, that's why Fritz has got to go back," Mom said. "I don't mind him killing mice, but if he killed a chipmunk and put it on the telephone stand, I couldn't bear it!"

She opened the Fannie Farmer box. "This will spoil our suppers," she said, "but what the heck." She took out a piece of candy for herself, one for Dad, and two for me. "I'm sorry, Davy," she said. I blushed brick red, but I ate the candy.

"OK, Fritz goes," Dad said. "But Charlotte, there's one thing I want to get straight. When you went to your closet the first time and discovered the candy was missing, you said you opened the box. Was the lid on it?"

Mom was at the stove, boiling some wieners. She looked back over her shoulder. "Yes, I'm sure it was," she said.

"Incredible," Dad said, and changed the subject.

After supper, he and I went down to the workshop in the basement. He hunted through a pile of scrap lumber until he found a slab of elm about an inch thick.

"I'll nail this over the hole in the paneling," Dad explained. "A beaver couldn't chew through old elm, let alone a chipmunk." He cut the slab to size and began to sand it.

"A remarkable animal is the chipmunk," he said, glancing over at me. "Your mother saw him in the closet, so we know that he found his way into the house, crawled behind the walls until he got to the closet, chewed through the paneling, took the lid off the box, and ate four pieces of candy."

"That much I can believe. What I can't believe is that he put the lid back on when he was through," Dad said. "Amazing, isn't it?"

He winked at me and went back to his sanding.

The Viggle Years

$\mathcal{I}$ can't remember the first fish I ever caught. It was probably a bluegill or perch that fell for an angleworm.

But I do remember the first largemouth bass. I could take you to the same lake tomorrow, find the same little bay, and cast to the same lily pad.

It was a Saturday morning in June 1951. Dad rowed a creaky rented boat across the flat calm of Hartlaub Lake, a thirty-acre pothole southwest of Manitowoc. Rosy light fanned over the horizon from the sunrise that was on its way.

Dad rounded a point and let the boat drift toward a lily pad bed on the east shore. He held a forefinger to his lips and pointed to my rod, meaning that I should pick it up, very quietly.

"Make an easy cast to the outside edge of the pads," Dad whispered. "Wait for the splash rings to go away. Count to thirty.

Then give the plug a jerk so it'll 'bloop' on the surface. Reel up the slack line. Wait for the rings to disappear. Count to thirty and bloop it again."

We drifted within a reasonable cast of the pads. I was pretty good with my trusty, solid-steel True Temper bait-casting rod and precious Pflueger Supreme reel. I swooshed the rod back and launched a ponderous, red-and-white Heddon Chugger plug toward the pads. It landed with a splat, almost on target. The rings disappeared. A puff of predawn breeze riffled the water. Twenty-eight, twenty-nine, thirty. Bloop!

Swirl! Hit! Bolts of lightning coursed up the line, down the rod, and into my hands. "Nail him!" Dad yelled, and I leaned back to set the hook.

Wow! This was no fussy little bait-stealing bluegill, but a fish with a mind of its own! Nothing Dad said during the sleepy drive from town had prepared me for a fish that actually fought back, that yanked the rod tip down into the water and pulled line off the Pflueger against the pressure of my thumb on the spool. Down, down he bored, and then shot to the surface, jumping clear of the water and shaking the hooks of the Chugger with a terrifying rattle.

But in a minute or two it was over. Dad scooped up the bass with a flick of the landing net, and I was face to face with sixteen inches of mean, green largemouth. My bass was only three times as long as the big cedar plug he had tried to eat. He wasn't Old Beelzebub, the ten-pound, bulge-bellied bass of my dreams, but as far as I was concerned he was the biggest fish in Wisconsin.

Dad popped the Chugger's massive hooks out of the bass's mouth. He handed the fish to me. I held it fearfully by the lower jaw and felt the prickles of its teeth.

"What d'you say we give him a second chance?" Dad asked. I

knew what that meant. I slipped the bass into the water and watched it flash out of sight.

My first bass, come and gone in about five minutes, only a memory. Loss and gain, pride and pain swirled around in my head. I had wanted that bass, and yet I didn't really want it dead. I glanced up at Dad. He was smiling at me, a steady smile of approval, man to man. I swallowed hard and felt the aching throat that comes before tears. But I wasn't a kid anymore. I was eight years old and had to take the rough with the smooth.

"Let's see if we can catch a bigger one," Dad said. And so we fished through our full battery of lures: the Chugger, a Bass-O-Reno, an Al Foss Oriental Wiggler with a pork frog on it, a Shannon Twin-Spin, a Creek Chub Pikie Minnow, a Jitterbug, a Flatfish, and a Pearl Wobbler made of genuine Ohio River clam shell. But by ten o'clock it was obvious that the bite was over. It was time to go home and mow the lawn.

Dad rowed back to the little landing where a farmer rented boats. He tossed the anchor, a coffee can full of concrete, up on the grass. We unloaded our rods and stood looking out over the lake. Dad thumbed some Walnut into his pipe, struck a match on the sole of his shoe, and lit it.

"This is a nice little lake," Dad said. "We'll have to come back some time."

But we weren't back—not for two years. The shipyard at Manitowoc was busier than ever, and Dad was the engineer who had to inspect construction and repairs. He started working six- and seven-day weeks. He'd leave before I got up in the morning and get home late, eating a warmed-up supper at the kitchen table, still wearing his dirty white coveralls. Men from the fabrication shop would call at two in the morning, demanding that Dad drive down to the yard to approve a weld or witness a hydrostatic test.

For the rest of that summer and all of the next, there was no time for Saturday mornings at Hartlaub Lake. I began to hate the shipyard, even though it put gas in the Studebaker and meatloaf on the table. Then the yard paid an odd dividend.

During the winter of '52–'53, Dad got to know the elderly Finnish chief engineer of a small ship that was laid up at the yard for repairs. The ship's captain and most of its crew headed home as soon as the boilers were cold, but the old chief, the cook, and the second mate were left behind as a skeleton force of shipkeepers. The cook and the second mate spent most of their time ashore at the Westfield Bar, but the chief preferred black coffee, fish stories, and his pipe. So did Dad, and before long he was eating most of his lunches and midnight snacks with the chief, who told tales of Finland's giant pike and salmon in broken, out-of-tune English.

One night in January, after a pot of eggshell coffee and a couple of corned-beef-and-onion sandwiches, the chief handed Dad a half dozen little cardboard boxes.

"Second engineer, he's coming back pretty soon, then I go home. You like to fish so you try these," the chief said.

The boxes held peculiar little minnow-shaped wooden fishing lures, painted blue above and white below, each with a U-shaped piece of celluloid under its chin. They didn't look like much to Dad, but the chief was enthusiastic.

"They made from balsavood," the chief said. "They float. You pull them, they go down and they . . ." He made a sinuous motion with his hand.

"Swim?" Dad said. "Wiggle?"

"Ya!" the chief laughed. "Viggle! A man in my town make them, catch big pike."

Dad didn't know it, but he had been given what might have been the first Rapala lures in North America, handmade in Finland by

Lauri Rapala. Millions of fish that had never seen a balsa minnow were waiting, stupid and hungry, for the first Rapala to viggle by. But a foot of ice covered those fish at the time, and Dad left the lures on his desk at the shipyard until May.

And then came a Saturday morning with no welding, shell plating, or tank tops to inspect.

Dad and I were back at Hartlaub Lake. We rented the same little boat with the same coffee-can anchor, the same leaks and squeaks. We tied two of the balsa minnows on our brand-new Shakespeare spinning rods and rowed over to the lily pads that were the scene of my victory two years before. We cast our minnows to opposite ends of the bed. We waited until the rings disappeared. We counted to thirty. We pulled the minnows down to make them viggle.

And Smash! Slurp! We each hooked a bass. After those two, there were two more. And then two more.

Imagine yourself an innocent farm boy who's at the circus for the first time. You blunder into the wrong tent and discover the beautiful bareback rider in the act of removing her tutu. You've never seen such a thing. She looks over her shoulder at you, tosses her long blonde hair, and crooks her finger. You know it's too good to be true, but you figure, what the hell.

That's the way the bass reacted to our balsa minnows that morning. The lonesome bass of Hartlaub Lake didn't just bite the Finnish vigglers, they slobbered over them. They knew they'd regret it, but it didn't stop them for a second.

Our first slow row around the lake yielded thirty-two bass. The second time around we caught seventeen more, along with a couple of walleyes and a pike of nightmare size. We let them all go.

Dad was counting. "Enough," he said. "That's forty-nine bass, and there's no point making pigs of ourselves for an even fifty. Besides, I've got a backlash here that's like the Sunday crossword— it'll take a week to work it out."

Dad picked up the oars and started to row back to the landing. "Cut off those vigglers and hide them in the tackle box," he said, "and tie on some Pikie Minnows. The farmer who rents the boats has been watching us, and I don't want him to see what we've really been using."

At the dock, the farmer was enthusiastic. "Jeez, you guys were really catching 'em, enso?" he said, all smiles. He looked carefully at the lures dangling from our rod tips. "Pikie Minnows, eh? Green Pikie Minnows. Well, well!"

After the farmer left Dad sat down on an overturned boat and lit his pipe.

"I have never, ever, had a day of fishing like this in my life, and neither have you, nor are you likely to again," Dad said. "If we'd kept all those bass, we would have cleaned out the lake. We've got to keep these vigglers quiet. Very quiet. Otherwise everybody will be wanting some."

And then began a halcyon time in our lives: the viggle years. Our vigglers caught bass on High Lake in Vilas County and just about everywhere else up north. They caught walleyes and muskies on the Big Chip. They caught giant crappies on the Mississippi. And there was a day among the smallmouth on the Red Cedar River that was absolutely obscene.

It wasn't hard to figure out what was happening. A fish is a simple soul, and if you show him a lure he's never seen, chances are he'll take a shot at it. But if he hits that lure and gets off, or watches other fish being caught on it, he'll think twice the next time it comes by. The fish we were catching had learned to avoid the big wooden plugs thrown at them by thousands of fishermen. In time they would learn to avoid vigglers, too. But it would take them a long time to learn about vigglers when only two fishermen had them.

By now you've guessed the drawback to all this success: We couldn't tell anybody about it. For awhile, Dad and I were probably the most productive fishermen in the state of Wisconsin, but we couldn't let on! It was awful. Other fishermen would see us catching fish; they'd ease over our way to see how we were doing it, and as soon as they'd get within a hundred yards, we'd have to cut off the vigglers and tie on something else, usually Pikie Minnows. It got to where we'd keep a pair of Pikie Minnows hanging on the gunwale of the boat, so they would be handy.

But it wasn't long before the gods of fish and fairness got their revenge. Our vigglers began to disappear. On one horrible day, two were stolen right off our rod tips at a boat landing. A month or so later, another was lost to a musky that simply overwhelmed us. Then a smallmouth bass the size of a sewer lid ran off with one in Jackson Harbor. After that, we fished the remaining two vigglers with heavy line and tuna-gauge wire leaders that killed their viggle.

The final blow was a stump on the bottom of the Manitowish River that claimed viggler number five during a bass fishing trip in 1956. We spent a half hour trying to pull it loose before the line finally snapped.

There was a brief period of silence. Then Dad cut the last viggler from the end of my line and held it up. "We should have kept a pair for seed," he said. "As it is, this guy's like the last passenger pigeon. He's extinct and doesn't know it."

The viggle years had come and gone. You can't fool all of the fish all of the time, and we were philosophers enough to understand that. But damn, it was tough to rejoin the ranks of ordinary unlucky fishermen.

The passing years brought their anodyne. As the fifties wore on, the shipyard stayed busy and Dad and I spent more time shooting and hunting. The last viggler hung in a place of honor from a joist in our basement workshop. The memories it called up were indelible and did not need enlargement.

And then, one day in 1959, Dad and I stopped at Sporting Goods Supply on Quay Street to pick up some shotgun powder, and Lloyd Bottoni pushed a couple of little cardboard boxes across the counter for us to look at. Inside were balsa minnow lures, each with a piece of plastic under its chin. Vigglers.

"These are the latest thing, Dave," Lloyd said. "Some guy in Finland makes them by hand and catches all kinds of fish with them. They're called Rapalas."

"But we had those . . . ," I blurted. Dad caught my eye and shook his head. I shut up. Dad bought two of them and picked up the powder.

Out in the car, we took the Rapalas out of their boxes. They were vigglers all right, painted black on top and gold on the bottom.

"Well, they aren't extinct anymore," Dad said.

"What's wrong with telling people we had them in 1953?" I asked.

"We would just be bragging," Dad said, "and pride goeth before destruction, and a haughty spirit before a fall. We had a run of good luck—let's leave it at that."

He lit his pipe. "This is one secret that's worth keeping," Dad said. "Save it for your memoir."

And so I did.

The Christmas
When a Lot Happened

Our Christmas of '52 began late in the evening on Monday, December twenty-second, lasted until the twenty-ninth, and was beyond a doubt the most action-packed week of my life up to that point. Events tumbled after each other so rapidly that when remembering them in later years, Mom, Dad, and I had to divide them into episodes.

"Do you remember the car ferry and the Saint Bernard?" one of us would ask, and we'd roll our eyes. "How about the Zoks and the hot pierogi? And the green brandy?" We'd begin a recital of our holiday stories, adding details and correcting errors as we went along. After a dozen tellings, the stories became polished chapters of family folklore, with titles, quotes, and punch lines.

The Crossing

I don't remember much about the Christmases of '50 and '51, except that they began and ended with two-day, five-hundred-mile drives from Manitowoc to Lorain and back again, through blizzards and snowdrifts that our bullet-nose Studebaker battled defiantly, its rear wheels spinning and flathead six whining.

There were no Midwestern turnpikes or interstate highways in the early '50s. When we drove from Wisconsin to Ohio for Christmas, we spent about half of each day scudding across windswept cornfields on two-lane blacktop roads, and the other half crawling in second gear through every town, city, and village along the way. That's where the highways went; there were no bypasses.

We'd leave Manitowoc before sunrise and drive through the middle of Sheboygan, Port Washington, Milwaukee, Racine, Kenosha, Waukegan, Evanston, and Chicago, arriving at Dyer, Indiana, at dark. There were three reasons for stopping at Dyer: it was about as far as Dad could drive in a day without slipping into a coma, it had a motel that met Mom's standards, and there was an Italian restaurant called the Olive Branch across the street from the motel, a friendly, garlicky place where we could unwind and fill up on spaghetti.

The next morning we'd make another early start, eat breakfast at a diner, and then creep across northern Indiana and Ohio, stopping for every traffic light in places like Ligonier, Butler, Bryan, Napoleon, Fremont, and Sandusky.

These treks aged Mom and Dad prematurely and took about a hundred bucks a year off the trade-in value of the Studie, which wasn't worth a lot to begin with. In 1952, confronted with another Christmas drive, they said no, no, never again. There had to be a better way.

So Dad decided to take the only available shortcut, the car ferry across Lake Michigan, from Manitowoc to Ludington. He had ridden the ferry a couple of times on business trips. We would board about eleven at night, he said, with the Studie safely stowed away below decks, and sleep our way across the lake in a comfortable stateroom. We'd arrive refreshed on the Michigan side early in the morning, pile into the car, and drive southeast across Michigan, saving a half day of driving and getting to Lorain about suppertime.

It was twenty above the night we left, with a damp, gusty northeast wind off the lake. When we got to the ferry dock we could hear waves thumping into the breakwall around Manitowoc's harbor. We boarded the ferry while railroad cars were being shunted aboard, leaving the Studie on the dock, to be loaded last. The staterooms were on the main deck surrounding a central passenger lounge; our room was about nine feet wide and had narrow upper and lower berths. The single porthole was iced over on the outside and didn't offer much of a view.

Once in the stateroom there was nothing to do but go to bed, so Dad boosted me into the upper berth and turned off the flickering, forty-watt overhead light so he and Mom could undress in privacy. With a certain amount of giggling and muttering, they squeezed themselves into the lower.

In the meantime I had discovered a curious feature at the head of my berth: a wickerwork ventilation panel through the bulkhead between the lounge and the stateroom. It was caned like a chair seat, with holes that let me see and hear the passengers who hadn't paid for a stateroom and were going to spend the night sleeping on sofas in the lounge. There were only three lounge passengers that night: a scrawny, harassed-looking man, his fat and dumpy wife, and their Saint Bernard dog.

I didn't pay much attention to the man and wife; what caught my eye was the Saint Bernard. I had never seen one in the flesh, and he exceeded my expectations, particularly in the amount of saliva he produced. He was a copious drooler, and when the engine started hammering and the ferry pulled out of its slip, the noise and vibration worried him and he drooled even more.

In a minute or two we cleared the breakwater and began to punch into big seas that had been rolling all the way from Michigan. The ferry would rise, hesitate, and then plunge down into the trough. There it would wallow for a few seconds and begin another slow rise. At the top of the next swell the bow would meet the oncoming crest and ram it with a boom that made the ferry shake.

None of us liked this, the Saint Bernard least of all. He shook his head back and forth, flinging ropes of saliva from his glistening jowls. A large stringy dollop landed on the fat lady's black wool overcoat. Her husband pulled a handkerchief from his back pocket and dabbed at it, but he couldn't keep up with the Saint Bernard, who seemed to be melting.

"Get that damn dog away from me!" the fat lady shouted. "It makes me sick to look at him!"

"All right, all right, all right," said the husband. He pulled the dog to the far end of the lounge and tied its leash to the metal frame of a big leather-covered sofa.

By this time we were a couple of miles out into the lake. The swells were farther apart now, and the ferry started to roll as well as pitch. The rolling panicked the Saint Bernard, and he headed back to his master, pulling the sofa behind him, his claws scrabbling on the linoleum.

But the fat lady had more than dog spit to worry about. The rolling and pitching were getting to her. Her face was fish-belly white and her eyes were open wide. She gave her husband a bruising poke in the ribs. "Herman! I'm going to throw up. Get something!" she yelled.

Herman jumped to his feet and looked around for a container.

He spotted a metal wastebasket at the forward end of the lounge and started for it, tottering on the pitching deck. And then the lights in the lounge went out. They were turned off at midnight to let the lounge passengers sleep.

"For God's sake, Herman, hurry up!" squalled the fat lady. Herman was a quick thinker; I heard the click of a Zippo and he reappeared, sliding back down the deck toward his wife, the wastebasket in one hand and his flaming cigarette lighter in the other. The fat lady grabbed the basket, stuck her head into it, and began to retch cavernously. She had apparently eaten a big supper—it smelled like sauerkraut and liverwurst, washed down with a couple of beers— and now it was all coming back.

In the flickering yellow light of the Zippo, I could see Herman's face. He was grinning. The rolling didn't bother him, and for once, I guessed, he had the upper hand. He fished a cigarette out of his shirt pocket and lit it. Suddenly there was a long whistling buzz. The fat lady was farting helplessly inside a girdle stretched tight as a drum-head by her mighty buttocks.

"Steady, Elsie," Herman said. "One end at a time." He was still grinning.

The Zippo went out and it was dark again. The Saint Bernard whined and Elsie moaned. Eventually I fell asleep.

When we left our stateroom the next morning, Elsie, Herman, and the dog had gone.

All that remained of them was the wastebasket, an odor of sauerkraut, and a yellow puddle with cigarette butts in it.

A few minutes later we climbed into the Studie and headed for Lorain. Mom looked over at Dad. "Never again," she said. "Do you hear me? Never again."

"Right," Dad said, and tamped his pipe, which had begun to go out.

Waiting for Puppa

"Puppa" was the nickname I gave my great-grandfather Albert when I was about four years old. Because I was the only great-grandchild on my mother's side of the family at the time, anything I said was clever, and the name stuck.

Puppa was a short, sturdy man with a full head of silver hair and a flowing salt-and-pepper mustache. He had been a building contractor in Detroit for most of his life, and kept on working until the outbreak of World War II, when he was about seventy. Then he cashed in his chips, left Detroit, and bought a tin-roofed house surrounded by orange trees near Lake George in central Florida.

Puppa and Great-grandma liked Florida but couldn't bear the idea of staying there for Christmas. During the war, when gasoline and tires were rationed, they took the train to Lorain each year to spend the holidays with their daughter Myra and their son-in-law Henry Lester, who were my maternal grandparents. Everyone gathered at Grandpa and Grandma's, and for many years we had four-generation Christmases.

After Great-grandma died, Puppa quit taking the train and started driving to Lorain for Christmas. With gasoline available again and selling for twenty-seven cents a gallon, he figured it was cheaper to take his '39 DeSoto than to squander money on a Pullman roomette. Also, he considered the car to be more direct.

"Damn railroad jumps all over the map, this way and that, gotta change trains three times and I can't get any closer than Cleveland," he said. "In the car I can go direct, pull out of my driveway, and right up yours." As far as Puppa was concerned, the intervening three days and nine hundred miles were a mere bagatelle.

Dad often wondered how Puppa navigated the southern backwoods without ever seeming to get lost. He found out one Christmas when he took a look at a highway map Puppa had left on the passenger seat of the DeSoto. Drawn on the map with a thick carpenter's pencil was a perfectly straight line from Lake George to Lorain. Puppa simply drove the roads that were closest to the line, a route that took him due north through Georgia and the moonshine country of South and North Carolina, over the Great Smokies, across the tag-ends of Tennessee, West Virginia, and Kentucky, and finally into Ohio. When Puppa said direct, he meant direct.

Grandma worried about Puppa's long drives. Year after year she tried to talk him into taking the train; year after year he refused. Her anxiety peaked around the twentieth of December each year, when Puppa would call long distance from Florida. He would place the call through the "central" operator on his local line, and then hang up and wait for central to call him back. Central would call the nearest long-distance operator, who passed the connection northward through a succession of additional operators, a process that could take as much as an hour. Once the line was open from Florida to Lorain, Puppa would get right down to business.

"Hi, Chickee." Chickee was his nickname for Grandma. "I'm leaving in the morning. Should get there on the twenty-third."

"Dad," Grandma would beg, "why don't you take the train this year? There's snow in the mountains and we really don't mind going into Cleveland to meet you."

"Nope, nope, too late now—I'll never get a ticket, and besides, the train jumps all over the map," Puppa would say. "Gotta hang up now, we've been talking a minute already." Puppa made long-distance calls with his pocket watch in hand. "See you on Tuesday. Good-bye." Click.

Besides Puppa's obsession with going direct, Grandma had another reason for worry: as a driver, Puppa was largely self-taught. He had bought his first car in 1922, when he was fifty years old. The salesman gave him a half-hour driving lesson, and from then on he was on his own.

Puppa had worked with machines all his life, so he had no trouble learning to operate a car. And he agreed with most of the traffic laws. He obeyed the speed limits, and at a four-way stop or a traffic light he would wait patiently, knowing that in a minute or two it would be his turn to go. He also understood that at certain intersections he would have to yield the right-of-way, and he tolerated that too, within reason.

When a side road he was on intersected a busier road, he would stop and look both ways like any careful driver. A car from the right would go by, then one from the left, and then another from the right, and Puppa would wait. But after about ten closely spaced cars had passed without letting him go, Puppa would lose his patience, muttering and tapping his clutch foot on the floorboards. He was willing to yield, but not forever.

"It's not fair!" Puppa would yell. "Those fellas just drive past like they don't even see me here. They won't give me a turn. Oh, the hell with it!" And he would pull out on the highway. So far, no one had hit him.

Dad had been right about one thing—the car ferry avoided the Chicago bottleneck and cut about twelve hours off our total elapsed time from Manitowoc to Lorain. The roads in Michigan and northern Ohio were clear, and the Studie cruised along at a steady fifty-five between towns, its snow tires humming. We arrived at Grandpa's in the early evening of the twenty-third. After we unpacked the car, Grandma served up bowls of chicken soup with dumplings the size of tennis balls. She took occasional sips of her soup, but spent most of her time pacing back and forth, watching the street through the dining room windows. She was waiting for Puppa, who was a couple of hours overdue.

"I have begged and I have pleaded, do not drive all the way from Florida at your age," she said, "but will he listen? No, he will not. A fine Christmas we'll have if he's dead in a ditch someplace. And now look!" she shouted. "It's starting to snow!"

Big flakes the size of silver dollars were falling, thick and wet, fluttering down in the glow of the streetlights. But I had faith in Puppa, so I dug into a plate of frosted cutout cookies Grandma had put on the table. I preferred the Santas and snowmen, because they were the largest, and I was on my fourth snowman when a pair of yellowish headlights pulled up the driveway.

"Oh my God, oh my God, is it him?" Grandma cried. "Henry, go and look. It's probably the police come to tell us he's dead!"

"It's him," Grandpa said. "Cops never drive DeSotos—they overheat."

Puppa came in through the kitchen door, stamping his feet and brushing his sleeves to shed the snow. His mustache and felt hat were frosted with it. "Hello, hello, hello," he said. "Merry Christmas. Do I smell chicken soup?" He lifted the lid of the kettle on the stove. "Hey, dumplings!" he said. "I'll have some in a minute, but I've got to run down to the drugstore before they close. I need some pipe tobacco. I ran out down around Coshocton." He gave me a meaningful look. "You coming, Davy?"

I put on my jacket, slipped out the door, and hopped into the DeSoto before Mom or Grandma could object. Puppa backed down to the sidewalk and started looking back and forth at the traffic on East Erie Avenue. In those days East Erie was also U.S. Highway 2, the principal route from New York to Chicago. Traffic was always heavy on U.S. 2.

"You look right and I'll look left," Puppa said. "Anybody coming?"

"Yes, yes," I said, hastily. "Lots of 'em."

Puppa glanced to the left. "How about now?" he asked.

"They're still coming," I said.

Puppa's left foot began to tap on the floorboard. "Now?"

"No!"

"The damn store will be closed before I can get out of here," Puppa said. He looked to the left again, stamped on the clutch, and shifted into reverse. "Oh, the hell with it," he said, and backed out.

To my knowledge I've never been closer to death than I was at that moment, when Puppa's DeSoto blocked both lanes of U.S. 2. The street was suddenly full of cars skidding silently on the wet snow. They went by in all directions. One car avoided us by driving up Grandpa's driveway. Another jumped the snowbank and wound up across the street on Mrs. Snell's sidewalk. A third spun and slid backward past my side of the car; the driver's face was plastered against the window, his mouth open, and his eyes round and frantic.

In a few more seconds it was all over. Puppa's luck had held and no one had hit anyone. "Damn you people!" Puppa shouted, from the safety of the DeSoto. "If you had given me a turn, you wouldn't have to slam on the brakes like that. Everybody knows you can't stop short on fresh snow!"

Puppa shifted into low and threaded his way through the jumble of cars. "I just hope the store's still open," he said.

We got there five minutes before it closed. Puppa asked the druggist for Blue Boar tobacco, which came in a glass jar. Then he reached down and ruffled my hair. "Find something you like," he said. There was a small display of toys and novelties: rubber base-balls, yo-yos, peashooters, and such. But all I could see was a chrome-plated cap pistol, a cap pistol to end all cap pistols, an exact copy of a snub-nosed Colt Detective Special .38 revolver. Best of all, it fired disc caps, which were three times as loud and twice as smoky as the caps that came in a roll.

Puppa saw me staring at the pistol. He picked it up and put it on the counter, along with an entire carton of disc caps. "You'll need some cartridges," he said. While I was admiring the cap pistol, he bought something else that he hid from me, slipping it into a paper sack with the Blue Boar.

On the way back to Grandpa's, Puppa turned on the radio. Fred Waring and the Pennsylvanians were singing a carol: "The world in solemn stillness lay, to hear the angels sing."

"Speaking of solemn stillness," Puppa said, "don't shoot that gun in the house—you'll scare your Grandma out of a year's growth. Chickee's a good girl but she's a great one for worrying."

The Advent of the Zoks

In the late afternoon of Christmas Eve, I was indulging in one of my favorite holiday customs, lying on my back with my head under the tree, looking up at the lights and ornaments, and savoring the scent of balsam.

On the Zenith console radio, Gene Autry was singing "Rudolph, the Red-Nosed Reindeer," and in the background I could hear the grownups talking—Mom and Grandma chatting in the kitchen, and Dad, Grandpa, and Puppa arguing war and politics in the dining room.

"Oh, sure, you're down on Eisenhower now, Albert," Grandpa said to Puppa, "but you thought he was pretty hot stuff on D-Day. It's about time we had somebody in the White House who'll settle their hash in Korea, and if we can't have MacArthur, Ike will do. Anything's better than Roosevelt or some damned necktie salesman like Truman."

Grandma was an ardent New Dealer and she had been listening from the kitchen. She strode into the dining room, her arms folded across her chest. "All right, Henry," she said, "you and Ike go and fight a war someplace. And when your Social Security checks start coming in, you just hand them over to me!"

This was getting interesting. I crawled out from under the tree and sat up so I could watch as well as listen.

"It's just too damn bad Ike had to saddle himself with Nixon," Puppa said. "I've had that sniveling little whelp pegged from the beginning. He's a crook, sure as hell. I tell you, it takes a pretty small man to hide behind a cocker spaniel!"

Dad laughed and Puppa banged his fist on the table. Puppa had been polishing this crack about Nixon's "Checkers" speech for weeks and was overjoyed to find an opening for it.

"Anyway," Puppa said, "getting back to the war—I never could figure out why they dropped that second A-bomb. One was enough. They should have saved the second one for the Russians."

"Russians, hell!" Grandpa said. "They should have dropped it on the Vatican!"

"Henry!" Grandma shouted from the kitchen. "Enough, for God's sake. It's Christmas Eve."

Then the doorbell rang. I went to the door and saw a big blond man standing on the front porch. He was about six foot six, with shoulders as broad as an axe handle, wearing a war surplus Navy pea coat. Behind him in the winter twilight was an old Chevrolet coupe pulled up tight against the curb. There was no room for parking on East Erie Avenue, and already cars were lining up behind the Chevy, honking and waiting for chances to get around.

"Let him in, Davy," Grandpa said. I did, and the man entered, stooping to clear the door frame. He stuck out a huge hand like the bucket of a dragline. Grandpa shook it and winced.

"Tanks," the man said in a gravelly bass voice. "Ludwik Zok from Gary, Indiana. My wife and I are going to Pennsylvania. I got flat on car and spare is flat too. You got phone I can call somebody to fix?"

51

"Sure," Grandpa replied, "but I don't think any of the filling stations will be open on Christmas Eve. Tell you what, I've got a pump and a patch kit and a tire iron. Let's get your car up the driveway and see if we can fix those flats ourselves. Myra, we've got company!"

There was a rush to put on overshoes and jackets. Slipping the clutch and driving slowly to take it easy on the flopping flat tire, Ludwik pulled the Chevy up the driveway and into the garage. I opened the passenger door to let Mrs. Zok out of the car and discovered a beautiful dark-haired woman with high Slavic cheekbones and penetrating blue eyes. She was tall and slender but, as kids my age used to say, she stuck out in front. Grandpa took one look and ran for help, pulling me along with him. In the kitchen, he was on the edge of panic.

"Myra, Charlotte!" he wheezed. "Get out there and help that woman. She looks like she's going to have a baby any minute!" Mom and Grandma looked at each other and headed for the garage without coats or boots. They soon reappeared, one on either side of Mrs. Zok. Supporting her by the arms, they guided her to a chair at the kitchen table and poured her a cup of coffee. Grandma ran cold water on a washcloth and held it to Mrs. Zok's forehead.

"I'm OK, I'm OK," she said, and laughed. "I got a week yet. My name is Elzbieta. Call me Lizzy."

She turned to me. "Go tell Ludwik to get pierogis from car, please. Nice Polish cabbage rolls. We have for supper, all right?" Out in the garage, the men had repaired one of the inner tubes and were blowing it up with the tire pump. Ludwik handed me a cardboard box full of doughy rolls shaped like little footballs and wrapped in waxed paper.

About a half hour later, both tubes were patched and the tires remounted. Dad, Grandpa, Puppa, and Ludwik came in from the garage just as the rolls were coming out of the oven. Ludwik smiled and rubbed his hands together. "Good. Pierogis. Hot. You like," he said.

Grandma set eight places at the kitchen table. Lizzy distributed the rolls—there were two apiece, as I remember—while Mom poured cups of coffee and glasses of milk.

We hesitated for a moment. None of us knew what to do with the pierogis. Finally Grandpa picked up a fork and Puppa instinctively reached for the Worcestershire sauce. "No," said Lizzy, "no fork, no sauce. Just bite." I picked up the larger of my pierogis and chewed off the end, releasing a cloud of steam.

Never in my life had I eaten anything as overwhelmingly seasoned as that pierogi. The first mouthful was like a slap in the face. A blast of red cabbage, sliced beef, yellow onion, horseradish, brown mustard, and Tabasco sauce hit the back of my throat and went up my nose. I coughed and chewed the cabbage. By the time I had swallowed, beads of sweat were breaking out on my forehead and my eyes were watering. Then came a powerful aftertaste, a fiery, beefy aroma that opened my sinuses and made the initial shock worthwhile. I had to have more of that, so I took a bigger bite, chewed, coughed, swallowed, and wiped the tears from my eyes with my shirtsleeve. Then I got the aftertaste again and smiled.

Everyone had been watching me. Ludwik laughed and slapped me on the back. "You like? Good? Eat more! Put hair on your chest!"

We felt obliged to clean our plates, so we struggled through our pierogis, gulping milk to keep our palates from blistering. When the last of the rolls had disappeared there was a collective sigh of relief and red cabbage.

"Lizzy, where is pie?" Ludwik asked. "I'll get it," Grandma said, rising from the table and fanning her face with her hand. She took a pie from the icebox—it had been in the cardboard box with the pierogis—and cut it into eight pieces, counting them with a fingertip to check her geometry. After the wrath of the pierogis, the pie was cool, sweet, and innocent. "Raisins, custard, and plum wodka," Lizzy said. "You want recipe?"

After the dishes were washed and the women had exchanged recipes and addresses, the Zoks asked for their coats. "Why don't you stay the night?" Grandma asked. "We've got a spare bedroom and a big turkey for dinner. We'd love to have you."

"And we like to stay," Ludwik said. "But we got five hundred miles to go. My brother got me good job at steel mill, got to start in three days." At the door there was an exchange of hugs and handshakes. Puppa blew his nose loudly and covered his face with his handkerchief. The Zoks went out the kitchen door and turned to say good-bye. Lizzy gave Mom a final hug.

"I say to Ludwik, we have no Christmas this year," Lizzy said. "But this was Christmas for us. This was Christmas."

Ludwik backed down the driveway and waited for a break in the traffic. Then he tooted the horn and headed east. We all stood on the porch and watched until the old Chevy disappeared down East Erie. It was quiet around the house after that.

"Stille Nacht"

But before long it was time to get dressed up and go to the Maryland Avenue Methodist Church for the Christmas Eve pageant. We all got into Grandpa's Packard and headed downtown through heavy snow that was blowing in off Lake Erie. It took a while to find a parking place big enough for the Packard, and by the time we got into the church all the pews in the sanctuary were full. We climbed the stairs to the rear balcony and found that we had it to ourselves.

"Good," Puppa said. "Up here, we can talk."

"Dad, be quiet," Grandma said. "It's starting."

The lights in the sanctuary dimmed, and the Reverend Jim Folz walked down the aisle and ascended the steps to the pulpit.

He was an unassuming country boy from Washington Court House, Ohio, and his nickname, never used to his face, was Just Folks.

He welcomed us all. "And now," he said, "it is my pleasure to introduce the Maryland Avenue Sunday School Singers!" There was a murmur of anticipation from the congregation. From our position above the rear of the church, we could hear the Sunday School teachers trying to sort the kids into rows. But the Singers had been cooped up in the church basement for an hour of rehearsal, and they had scores to settle first. There were angry whispers from kids who were being poked or pinched.

"Ow!"

"Cut it out!"

"Damn you, Floyd!"

It was all clearly audible. Dad laughed out loud and Puppa snickered. Up in the pulpit, Just Folks tried to look serious but couldn't fight off a smile. Finally relative silence fell and we heard the toot of a pitch pipe.

"Up on the housetop, reindeer pause . . . ," the children sang, and started reluctantly down the aisle. It took all three verses of the carol to get them lined up in the chancel, just in front of the nativity scene and the Christmas tree. One of the teachers blew the pitch pipe again and the Singers launched into "Away in a Manger."

During the first verse, the congregation relaxed and smiled indulgently as the piping voices filled the church. But their faces froze as another Christmas tradition began to unfold.

A little girl in the front row, terrified by all the people looking at her, grabbed the hem of her dress and began to twist it around and around. As we watched she wound it higher and higher, revealing her chubby legs and white underpants. Soon her stomach and navel were uncovered.

"I love thee, Lord Jesus, look down from the sky . . . ," sang the children.

"I hope he isn't looking down at *her*," Grandpa said.

"I could swear it's the same girl that pulled up her dress last year," Dad said.

"She'd better outgrow that by the time she's sixteen or so," Puppa whispered. "It could get embarrassing."

I glanced at Grandma. I expected to see her looking daggers at Puppa, but instead she had covered her eyes with one hand and was giggling like a schoolgirl. Mom's face was red, and she was giggling even louder than Grandma. I was astounded and a little scared. With Mom and Grandma out of action, discipline was sure to collapse. What sort of chaos would follow, I wondered, if Puppa got off another good one and there was no one to quiet us down?

We fought to regain straight faces as the children finished their last carol and retreated from the chancel. Just Folks gave them a few minutes to find their parents and squeeze into the pews.

"And now," he said, "let's sing 'Angels from the Realms of Glory.'" The organ played a four-bar introduction and the congregation sang while two high-school girls marched down the aisle and took up positions behind the manger. They wore wings made of cardboard and tinfoil and halos of tinsel and coat-hanger wire.

Mary and Joseph were next, followed by three boys wearing gaudy bathrobes and carrying cigar boxes daubed with gold paint. Then Mary removed a large, blond doll from her robes and placed it in the manger. "Ma-ma," it said. Grandma started giggling again.

"Gerald Jones will present the reading for this evening, from the Gospel According to Luke," Just Folks said. A gangling boy in a blue pin-striped suit walked solemnly to the lectern, opened the big bible, and began to recite.

"And Joseph also went up from Galilee, out of the city of

Nazareth, into Judea, unto the city of David, which is called Bethlehem, to be taxed with Mary his exposed wife, being great with child . . ."

Now all of us were giggling and snorting. "I knew she was expecting," Puppa whispered, "but I didn't think she was exposed." We weren't the only ones who thought it was funny. Below us in the sanctuary, a titter of laughter was passing up one pew and down the next. Finally, out of respect for Saint Luke, we shut up as Gerald finished the reading.

"Glory to God in the highest, and on earth peace, good will toward men."

The pageant was almost over. Just Folks went to the altar, removed a single candle, and walked slowly down the aisle. "Silent night," he sang in a sweet tenor, "holy night."

Everyone stood and joined in. Puppa put his hand on my shoulder and began to sing softly in German:

Stille Nacht, heilige Nacht,
Alles Schläft, einsam wacht . . .

I looked up at Puppa. There were tears in the corners of his eyes. "Stille Nacht" had been Great-grandma's favorite carol.

Schlaf in himmlischer Ruh,
Schlaf in himmlischer Ruh.

It was Just Folks's custom to stand on the porch and shake hands with every member of the congregation as they went out the door. We were the last to leave, and his face lit up when he saw us.

"Myra, Henry!" he said. "Good to see you. And Dave and Charlotte, and little Dave, and Albert! The whole family is here."

"Thank you, Reverend Folz," Grandma said. "It was a very inspiring service."

"More amusing than inspiring, I think," Just Folks said. "I must inform young Gerald of the difference between 'espoused' and 'exposed.' I can't blame people for laughing. Or giggling."

He gave Grandma a smile. "It all goes under the category of making a joyful noise, I guess."

Grandpa was a sharp-edged, self-made man who usually went to church only when close friends were being married or buried. But he shook hands firmly with Just Folks, and handed him a twenty-dollar bill. "Put this in the plate for me on Sunday, will you, Jim?" he said. "Tonight was worth every penny."

"Merry Christmas!" said Just Folks.

"Merry Christmas!" we said, and shuffled through the snow to the Packard.

Christmas morning, we all got up early. Grandma and I were standing in the hall, waiting our turns to use the bathroom. There was a flush and Puppa came out.

"My God, Chickee," Puppa said. "I wonder what that woman put in those rolls. It was like passing razor blades!"

"Dad!" Grandma said, and jerked her head toward me. "Little pitchers."

"Well, it was," Puppa said. "The good news is, yesterday I thought I was coming down with something, but I'm OK now."

In the afternoon Grandma invited Mrs. Smith, a widow who lived next door, to come over for coffee and cookies. Mrs. Smith had seen the Zoks come and go and was consumed with curiosity. Grandma told her the story.

"Well, Myra," Mrs. Smith said, "all I can say is that it was pretty brave of you to take those people in like that. Heaven knows what they might have done!"

"Oh, Edna, I didn't worry," Grandma said. "They came in off the street on Christmas Eve, the woman pregnant out to here. And they were going to Bethlehem."

"Bethlehem?"

"Bethlehem, Pennsylvania. I tell you, Edna, it was like an omen. It was like a sign!"

Green Brandy

Back in the 1940s and '50s Grandpa got a lot of booze for Christmas. In those days, businesses could deduct gifts to their customers as expenses. If a salesman found out that a customer liked Haig & Haig Pinch Bottle scotch, for instance, a couple of fifths of Pinch would be dispatched to his home just before Christmas.

The same went for cigars. One of Grandpa's friends, a buyer for a hardware chain, received salesmen in his paneled office in the Terminal Tower, Cleveland's only skyscraper at the time.

"Henry," he said, "I've got it down to a science. I really like Montecristo cigars—you know, the Cuban ones that come in glass tubes and wrapped in cedar. I can't afford them as a regular thing, but every year in November I get an empty Montecristo box from the cigar store and leave it on my desk where the salesmen can see it when they come around. Sure enough, every Christmas it rains Montecristos."

Grandpa was the fleet engineer for a line of Great Lakes ore boats. He had to sign off on the purchase of everything from giant bronze propellers to buckets of grease, and he was hounded by salesmen every day. He was too honest to hint at presents, so the salesmen sent him pens, pencils, and an assortment of liquor every year, figuring that an executive in the marine trade would be sure to do a lot of writing and a lot of drinking.

But Grandpa didn't drink, and over the years he accumulated one of the largest cellars in northern Ohio, along with enough gold-plated mechanical pencils and fountain pens to arm a regiment of insurance agents. He gave most of the pens and pencils away, but he refused to hand out the unwanted liquor to his friends, fearing that it would enslave them. The day after Christmas every year, Grandpa made about a dozen trips to the fruit cellar in the basement, putting the new bottles on the shelves beside Grandma's home-canned relishes, chili sauce, tomatoes, and peaches.

I started to play with the liquor when I was five or six, before we moved to Manitowoc. It was always cool in the fruit cellar, and I spent many long summer afternoons there, arranging the bottles by brand and spelling out their fascinating names—Kummel, Goldwasser, Wild Turkey, Grant's Standfast, Vat 69, Jägermeister, Spey Royal, Glenfiddich. It was fun to hold the bottles up to the light and study their colors.

In time I began to open the bottles, sniffing the contents and mixing them together to see what would happen. Aalborg Aquavit, for instance, when mixed half-and-half with Martini and Rossi sweet vermouth, produced a blend with a scent of herbs and anise and a tawny brown color. Yellow liqueurs like Galliano created pleasant golden shades when mixed with vodka or gin. Once I blended a red liqueur with a white one. Shaken up, the mixture was a bright bubble-gum pink. By the next day it had separated into red and white layers, teaching me a little about specific gravity. A failed experiment involved the dilution of Three-Star Hennessey brandy with a liqueur called Chartreuse. The result was a bilious green fluid that looked like algae.

I broke off my experiments abruptly one summer morning when I read through a liquor ad in the Cleveland *Plain Dealer*. I recognized the names of many of my old friends from the fruit cellar. Then I had a shock; some of those old friends were selling for as much as four dollars a bottle. I decided to quit while I was ahead and undetected. But my researches in the fruit cellar came back to haunt me with the visit of Captain Tomlin on Christmas Day.

The captain and his wife showed up on the doorstep in the early evening, when Dad, Grandpa, Puppa, and I were in the living room, dozing off the aftereffects of too much turkey, too much dressing, and too much mincemeat pie and ice cream.

I was lying on the floor in front of a fire in the fireplace, flipping through a leather-bound illustrated history of the Civil War in three volumes, given to me for Christmas by a friend of Mom's named Cynthia. Cynthia was a nervous and distracted woman who was suffering through life as a high-school librarian. We found out later that she had put the wrong labels on some of the Christmas gifts she sent out that year; the three-volume history was intended for the principal of her school. We could only wonder what the principal thought when he opened his package and found a slender copy of *Mike Mulligan and His Steam Shovel.*

I was looking at pictures of the siege of Vicksburg when the doorbell rang. Grandpa groaned and struggled to stand up. Tightening his tie and slipping his suspenders back on his shoulders, he peered out one of the front windows to see who it was.

"Oh, Christ," he said, "it's Tomlin the ancient mariner and his tugboat. Myra," he shouted, "front and center! The Tomlins are here!"

Tomlin was a retired Great Lakes captain who had once been the skipper of an ore boat on which Grandpa was the chief engineer. Grandpa did not get along with captains as a class, and Carl Tomlin was no exception.

"It's all very well for Tomlin to sit around the pilothouse in a starched shirt, drinking coffee and watching the wheelsman do all the work," Grandpa used to say. "But he's not going to move a damned inch if I don't get steam up!"

The Tomlins were well known in Lorain as freeloaders and insufferable bores. But it was Christmas, so Grandpa sighed and let them in. Tomlin was a chubby man with thinning gray hair, flabby cheeks, and a protruding lower lip that gave him the look of a pouting bulldog. His wife was gaunt and hatchet faced and wore enough makeup to frost a cake.

"Henry, I hope you don't mind us dropping in like this," Tomlin said. "We were just driving by and saw your lights on."

"Not at all, Carl, not at all. Merry Christmas," Grandpa said, forcing a smile. Grandma invited Mrs. Tomlin into the dining room for coffee. Mom joined them and the three women sat down and began to talk. Tomlin headed for Grandma's chair by the fireplace, but Puppa cut him off.

"Don't sit there, Captain Tomlin," Puppa said, gripping him by the arm. "It's too hot. Here, take Henry's chair. Would you like a drink?"

"Thanks, Albert, I don't mind if I do," Tomlin said. "Some brandy would be good, if you have it."

"Oh, we have it," Puppa said, smiling in a way that made me suspect that he, too, knew his way around the fruit cellar. "Would Three-Star Hennessey suit you?"

An electric charge ran up my spine. There were at least five bottles of Hennessey in the cellar. As Puppa went down the basement stairs I prayed that he would bring up a fresh one and overlook the algae. But my prayer was not answered. In a few minutes Puppa came back into the living room, carrying a small glass filled to the brim with the cloudy green slop I had made in 1948.

Puppa handed Tomlin the glass. Tomlin took a sip, made a face, and swallowed with an effort.

"How is it, Captain Tomlin?" Puppa asked. "Oh, it's fine," Tomlin said, "it's just a little . . . sweeter than I expected." He took another sip, put the glass on an end table, and began to tell a tiresome story set in the days when he and Grandpa had been, as he imagined it, "old shipmates." Grandpa set his jaw and said nothing, determined

62

to tough it out. After a while the kaffeeklatsch in the dining room broke up and the women came into the living room.

"Come, Carl, we must be going," Mrs. Tomlin said.

"Oh, don't go yet, Mrs. Tomlin," Puppa said. "It's cold outside. Have a seat in Myra's chair by the fire and warm up a bit."

Mrs. Tomlin lowered herself into the chair in a ladylike fashion, but as soon as her angular bottom compressed the seat there was a loud, flubbering report. Mrs. Tomlin shot up from the chair as though propelled by springs.

Grandpa and Grandma stood motionless with their mouths half open. Mrs. Tomlin clenched her fists in fury and flushed so red you could see it through her makeup. Captain Tomlin gestured and sputtered. I tried to keep a straight face, with the memory of Elsie's explosion still fresh in my mind. And Puppa stood in the corner by the Christmas tree, smiling inscrutably like an elderly Buddha with a mustache.

He caught my eye and gave me a big wink. It dawned on me: the mysterious purchase at the drugstore had been a whoopee cushion, and Puppa had planted it in the chair. He had intended it to be a practical joke on Grandma, but when a target of opportunity like Mrs. Tomlin came along he couldn't resist.

"Carl! I said we are going!" Mrs. Tomlin shouted. Mom got the Tomlins' coats out of the closet. The captain was still sputtering. "How dare you . . . old shipmates . . . insulted my wife . . . never speak to you again!"

"Fine with me!" Grandpa said. And like the down of a thistle, the Tomlins flew out the front door, slamming it so hard the clock on the mantel struck six o'clock two minutes early.

Grandma went to her chair, removed the whoopee cushion, and threw it into the fire. "Well, we'll never see them again," she said. "Dad, I suppose this was your doing."

"Guilty," Puppa said. "Come on, Chickee, you know you hate

that old dragon. I saw your face when she walked in. You're well shut of her."

"Your father's right," Grandpa said. "Getting rid of that pair is like a second Christmas, let's face it."

I was taken aback by this sudden insight into adult life. I had been taught to be polite to everybody, even people I couldn't stand. But if you were grown up, apparently it was OK to be honest from time to time, if you were prepared to take the consequences.

Mom's voice came from the kitchen. She knew how to calm the fierce rush of life at Grandpa's. "Who wants a snack?" she asked. We sat down in the living room as she poured coffee and passed out cookies and turkey sandwiches. Then she opened the bench of Grandma's Mason and Hamlin upright piano and took out a book of Christmas music. "Play for us, Mom," she said.

Grandma had been a theater organist in the days of silent movies. Not only could she play, she could also improvise. Fugues and variations flowed from her hands as the spirit moved her. With the coming of talkies she played only to relax, and that night it took her about an hour. We sat silently in the living room, listening and watching by the light of the Christmas tree.

I was headed for bed when Puppa tapped me on the shoulder.

"I poured that green stuff down the drain," he said, "so it won't trouble us anymore. Oh, and another thing—are you really going to read those Civil War books?"

"Sure," I said.

"Good," he said. "Next Christmas you can tell me how it all comes out."

Yellow Dog Blues

On the morning of the twenty-eighth we got up at five thirty to pack the car for the trip back to Manitowoc. Grandma stirred up pancake batter while Dad and I carried luggage and presents out to the Studie. Our suitcases filled most of the backseat, leaving only a cubbyhole for me. Mom's job was to pack the trunk, and she pursed her lips in concentration as she moved the packages around to get a perfect fit.

We knew we wouldn't be together as a family until next Christmas, so it was hard to break away. But finally Dad looked at his watch and stood up. "Charlotte, Davy, let's go," he said. "We were supposed to be on the road by six thirty and it's seven already. I'll just take a walk around the house and make sure we haven't forgotten anything."

"Don't bother," Mom said. "I've already checked."

After a final round of good-byes we got into the Studie and Dad backed down the driveway. Traffic was light at that time of the morning and we had to wait only a couple of minutes for an opening. We pulled out and headed west, waving until Grandpa's house was out of sight.

"Well, that was quite a Christmas, all in all," Dad said. He and Mom talked about Puppa, the Zoks, and the Tomlins while I read the introduction to volume one of my Civil War books. The author spent a lot of time setting the scene. I plowed through the Missouri Compromise, the Wilmot Proviso, Bloody Kansas, and the Lincoln-Douglas debates before I fell asleep. When I woke up we had driven about a hundred miles. Dad was calling me.

"Davy, look around back there and see if you can find my pipe satchel," he said. Dad usually traveled with six pipes, which he carried in a kind of leather wallet with loops to hold them. That morning he had been smoking a Kaywoodie Canadian that Grandpa had given him for Christmas, but after the fourth smoke of the morning it was time to give it a rest and start a fresh pipe.

I moved the suitcases around. "I don't see it," I said.

"Charlotte, did you pack it in the trunk?" Dad asked.

"I don't remember," Mom replied. "The pipes are your failing."

"Yes, but you said you looked around the house before we left," Dad said. "Didn't you see the satchel? I think it was on the dresser."

"Well, then, it's still there," Mom said. "Anyway, you have your new pipe."

"But I can't smoke it for two days straight!" Dad said.

"Then maybe you shouldn't smoke so much," Mom said. "It will be nice to drive for a while without smoke in the car."

"Dammit, Charlotte, you know when I'm smoking I always roll my window down!"

"And that's another thing," Mom said. "What's the point of having a heater in a car if you drive with the window open all the time?" When Mom got stubborn she was an immovable object.

"OK, when we stop for gas I'll get a pack of cigarettes," Dad said. "Some day I may quit smoking, but I'm not going to do it in Indiana!" His pipe had gone out and he laid it on the dashboard. He looked at the gas gauge, settled himself in his seat, and began to drive a little faster.

Mom and Dad didn't argue very much, but over the years I had learned to judge the severity of their disputes by the tone of their voices. I had been listening intently, and this sounded like a pretty bad one. No one said a word for about twenty-five miles.

After a while I got tired of reading and began to play with my cap pistol. As we drove along I pointed it at cows, horses, and farmers we passed. I was sitting on Mom's overnight case to get a better view from the backseat, and looking ahead, I saw a big yellow dog waiting for us in a driveway on the left side of the road. He was a classic farm dog, a hundred-pound blend of shepherd and collie with a mane like a lion.

As I suspected, he was also a car chaser, and as we got closer he ran parallel to us in the opposite lane. Then he lunged at our front tire and Dad swerved to miss him. The Studie's right rear fender hit a snow bank and we spun lazily to the left. Dad sawed at the wheel to fight the skid. While all this was happening, his pipe slid off the dash and dumped black ashes on Mom's major Christmas present, a heather-mixture tweed coat.

"Now look what you've done!" she yelled as Dad got the car straightened out. She rolled her window down and wound up to throw the pipe out of the car. But at the last second she hesitated. Loathsome as it might be, the pipe was a gift from her father. She brushed the ashes from her coat and put the pipe into her purse, snapping the clasp firmly.

Dad needed a smoke. "Charlotte, give me that pipe," he said.

"No," said Mom.

Nothing was said for a half hour. I couldn't stand it any longer.

"Wanna hear a joke?" I asked.

"Fire away," Dad said.

"Puppa told it to me," I said. "There's this farmer and he has three daughters who are all trombone players . . ."

"I don't want to hear it," Mom said.

It was quiet again until we stopped for gas. At the filling station, Dad bought a pack of Camels. Back in the car, he started the engine and tore the cellophane off the package.

Mom stared at him. "Apparently you can't go a measly eight hours without smoking, can you?" she said.

"Yes I can!" Dad shouted. He rolled down his window and threw the cigarettes into the snow. Then he floored the gas and popped the clutch. The snow tires squealed as the Studie lurched out onto the highway. It took a heavy foot to make a Studebaker peel rubber in cold weather.

Nothing more was said, mile after mile. When we got to Dyer, Dad checked into the motel and carried the suitcases to our cabin.

67

Then he flopped on the bed and closed his eyes. Ten minutes went by, then twenty, then a half hour. Finally Mom was forced to speak.

"Dave, we'd better go over and eat before they close," she said.

"Great," Dad said, "let's go." Mom didn't need nicotine, but she did need supper. Dad had starved her out.

The Shootout in Dyer

The Olive Branch was in an old stone building that had once been a bank. It had terrazzo floors and marble walls and was a perfect echo chamber; if you dropped a plate in that restaurant, it sounded like a train wreck. We ordered and sat back to wait for our spaghetti. Mom and Dad were talking rather stiffly, looking at the wine list, and wondering what Asti Spumante was. I slipped my cap pistol out of my jacket pocket and began to fiddle with it under the table.

To this day I cannot understand how the pistol came to be loaded. Even at the age of ten I knew better than to bring a loaded gun indoors or to put my finger on the trigger until I was ready to shoot. But cap pistols are not built to the standards of Colt or Smith & Wesson. Somehow the hammer fell and the bang of the cap reverberated around the restaurant.

There were screams and instant hubbub. This was, after all, an Italian restaurant in the Chicago suburbs. There were about twenty other customers, and they all ran like rabbits. Some headed for the front door, some scuttled into the restrooms, others disappeared into the kitchen.

The owner burst in from the bar, his hands over his head in surrender, shouting, "Wotta hell, wotta hell?" Then he looked at us. As the only people still sitting down, we were either deaf or guilty. Dad reached under the table and pulled the pistol away from me. Wisps of smoke were still coming out of its barrel. He held it out to the owner, butt first. "Cap gun," he said.

The owner laughed in relief and wagged a finger at me. "Badda boy," he said. He bent down and whispered to Dad. Dad pulled out his wallet and handed over a ten-dollar bill.

Hearing no more shots, the customers came back into the dining room. When they had returned to their tables, waiters walked in from the bar bearing pitchers of Schlitz. Soon everyone was smiling and laughing and drinking beer. Glasses were raised to us all around, and we returned the toasts with sips of our Cokes.

"Schlitz on draft, good will to men," Dad said, and then looked at me. "That ten bucks is coming out of your snow-shoveling money." But I didn't think he really meant it.

Back at the motel, Dad took the cap pistol out of his pocket and tossed it into his suitcase. "I'll keep it safe in here until we get home," he said. "If that thing went off in the car I'd lose control altogether."

"And I'd wet my pants," Mom said. She gave me a playful swat on the backside and turned down the sheets on my bed. Things were mending. I fell asleep reading about the Battle of Shiloh.

The Viscount

Dad was used to smoking a pipe before breakfast, but the next morning his Kaywoodie was still shut away in Mom's purse and he wasn't about to beg for it. In the diner where we had breakfast, he paused by the cigarette machine, dug into his pocket for a quarter, and then clenched his teeth and walked on.

As we drove north through Gary I was fascinated by the colorful smoke boiling up from mills and factories: red, yellow, green, brown, orange. In Manitowoc the air sometimes smelled of roasting barley from Rahr Malting, but it was otherwise bland and invisible.

On the south side of Chicago there was less smoke but people were really crowded together. We drove past miles of three-story houses about twenty feet across, fronted with tiny lawns six feet on a side and separated by narrow alleys barely wide enough for a garbage can. As a kid with an acre of grass to mow, I wondered why the people who lived in those houses bothered with lawns at all. And how did they cut them? Did each block chip in on a lawnmower and pass it around from house to house? Or did they clip the grass with scissors?

When we entered the Loop, I wished as always that we could stop and walk around like small-town people, looking in the show windows of the stores and rubbernecking at the tall buildings. I always begged Dad to stop, but he never did. "We can't spare the time," he would say. "We'd get lost," Mom would say. "We'd get robbed!" Dad would say. When we drove through Chicago, we locked the car doors.

So I was surprised when Dad turned onto Wabash Avenue and parked the Studie. "Where are you going?" Mom asked. "Never mind," Dad said. "I'll be back in twenty minutes."

He crossed the street and entered a store. Over the door was a sign: Iwan Ries—Tobacconist Since 1857. "Oh, for God's sake!" Mom said.

I demanded to get out of the car. "My feet are asleep," I said. "I just wanna stand on the sidewalk."

"I suppose," Mom said, and rummaged in her purse. "Here, put this nickel in the parking meter, but don't go any farther!"

Finally, I had set foot in Chicago. I put the nickel in the meter and enjoyed the brisk whirring sounds it made as it digested the coin. It was a lot better than Manitowoc's flimsy little parking meters. Then I stared at the Chicagoans passing by. There was a distinguished-looking man wearing a hat I recognized as a Homburg, and a woman with the longest legs I had ever seen, the seams of her nylons perfectly straight.

When Dad came back he was smoking a huge, curve-stemmed pipe. I scrambled into the backseat and Dad got behind the wheel, puffing away. He rolled down his window.

"Everybody ready?" he asked, cheerily. Mom said nothing. Dad handed me the box the pipe had come in. Stamped on it were expensive-sounding words: Sasieni, Four Dot, London Made, Patent No. 150221/20, Viscount Lascelles. Cripes, I thought, this pipe is so ritzy it doesn't have a crummy model number like a Kaywoodie, it has four names and a patent!

Dad kept the big pipe going until we were well into Evanston. When it finally went out, he pulled over and used a shiny new pipe tool to loosen the dottle. He tapped the ashes into the street and carefully put the pipe in his shirt pocket.

We ate an early supper in a burger joint in Milwaukee. When it got too dark to read I fell asleep and didn't wake up until we were pulling out of Sheboygan. Soft music was playing on the radio and Dad was driving left-handed, his right arm around Mom and her head on his shoulder. Reflected in the windshield I could see the embers in his pipe, glowing red when he puffed. Christmas was merry again.

The next morning Dad and I drove out to Halvor Halvorson's farm where we had boarded our beagles. I worked up the nerve to ask Dad a personal question.

"I thought you didn't like curved pipes. How come you bought that one?"

"I bought it," he said, "because it was the most expensive pipe in the store. Sasieni is one of the best English makers, maybe the best. The Four Dot is their top of the line, and the Viscount Lascelles is about the biggest. Stupid thing to do—cost me almost a day's pay."

"I don't expect you to understand this," Dad said, "but I bought that pipe to spite your mother. Now I wish I hadn't. Last night I put it on the mantelpiece in the dining room where I can see it, and whenever I get mad at her, I'll look at that pipe and remember that I can be as big a fool as anybody."

That was my second glimpse of the grown-up mind in a couple of days. Adults were definitely more complicated than I thought.

When we got home from Halvor's, Mom set places at the dining room table and brought in the percolator and a plate of coffeecake just out of the oven.

"Funniest thing," she said, as she poured the coffee. "After you left to get the dogs this morning I unpacked my suitcase. You'll never guess what I found!" And she handed Dad his pipe satchel.

Dad didn't say anything. He was looking at the Viscount.

The Digging Out of Nip

It's funny how you find out about life.

You pick up a lot from your mother, your dad, and your wife, of course. It's their job to teach you things. But it pays to keep your eyes and ears open all the time. You learn some of the most important lessons by accident. For example, I learned about the value of friendship from the digging out of Nip on New Year's Eve 1953.

When we moved to Manitowoc in 1950, our nearest neighbors were forests and fields, a ravine and creek, a dairy farm, and Tony.

Tony, his wife, Mildred, a springer spaniel named Mickey, and Tony's pack of beagles lived next door. Tony and Mildred were the epitome of neighbors: friends who would give you their shirts in a pinch, and iron them first.

The matriarch of Tony's beagle pack was a little bitch named Susie, and sometime in 1951 a marriage was arranged between Susie and our beagle, Rip. The pick of the litter was a pup I called Nip, my personal beagle. Nip inherited Rip's pedigreed looks and singing voice, and Susie's vast reserves of face-licking affection and rabbit savvy.

Besides Susie and her beagle clan, Tony had another great asset: the only television set in the neighborhood. Back in 1953, only two channels "came in" around Manitowoc, one from Green Bay and the other from Milwaukee. The programs weren't much, as I remember: mostly *Hopalong Cassidy, Howdy Doody,* and wrestling.

Even as a kid I thought *Howdy Doody* was pretty stupid, and it didn't take long to get tired of watching Hoppy chase the same villains around the same twenty acres of Southern California. But the wrestling was just what the doctor ordered, a mild sedative for people who had put in a long day.

There were no flashy costumes or shaggy haircuts. The wrestlers were big, tough Italians and Irishmen who wore high-top sneakers, skimpy little black underpants, and tattoos with simple messages like "USMC" and "Mother." Each match was a melodrama of good versus evil with plenty of slapstick thrown in, an irresistible combination, and Dad and I didn't resist. On wrestling nights, we were regulars in Tony's TV den.

Tony and Dad would sprawl in easy chairs while Mickey and I lay on the rug. Tony would put out a big bowl of Kraft caramels, and we'd eat them by the dozens while glued to the screen. During commercials Tony would pick the cellophane from five or six caramels, squeeze them into a ball, and toss them to Mickey. Dogs' teeth are not made for eating caramels; it takes a dog quite a while to dispatch even one, and Mickey could make a half dozen last a good five minutes, drooling and wagging his stub of a tail while he took savage bites. Some nights, Mickey's struggles with the caramels were better than the wrestling.

It was on one of these wrestling nights that Tony suggested the final rabbit hunt of the year.

"I want to get the beagles out one more time before it gets too damn cold," Tony said to Dad. "Gotta work tomorrow morning, so how about tomorrow afternoon? It's New Year's Eve, but I'm not going anyplace." As fifth-generation Methodists, our family never had plans for New Year's Eve, and so the hunt was on.

Saturday dawned cold and clear. By midmorning, a stiff northwest wind was shuffling the drifts of dry, fluffy snow in our yard. Dad muttered and scraped frost off the kitchen window to get a look at the thermometer. "Ten above," he said, shaking his head. "Tony must be nuts."

I didn't care how cold it was. After an hour of wheedling the night before, I'd convinced Dad to let Nip and me come along. We'd be serving only as observers; at eleven, I was too young to carry a gun, and Nip was still a half-grown pup with a high tenor voice. But we were finally going to go rabbit hunting with the grown-up men and the grown-up dogs! I was light-headed with impatience.

Late that morning, mighty preparations began. Mom perked a pot of coffee and poured it into our fragile glass thermos. Dad rooted through dresser drawers in search of long johns and thick wool socks. He took his Lefever shotgun from the cabinet and put it in its case. His Bass Trailmaster boots got a coat of mink oil to keep out the snow.

I put on long underwear, two pairs of socks, flannel-lined jeans, a wool shirt, my kid-sized army snorkel parka, five-buckle galoshes, and deerskin choppers with scratchy mittens inside. Dad snapped the leashes on Rip and Nip, and we plowed through the snow to Tony's house.

I don't remember much about the ride to Tony's number one rabbit cover, a hundred-acre woods near Millhome in the Town of

Schleswig. Dad and Tony rode in front, smoking and scraping ice off the inside of the windshield. Six beagles and I had the backseat to ourselves.

But the excitement was thick as Tony's car eased to a stop on a narrow road through the woods. I opened a back door, releasing a torrent of beagles. Dad and Tony loaded their guns with dark red Winchester shells, and we were off, the dogs fanning out before us.

For an hour we trudged. An hour and a half. After two hours of briar patches, cattails, and alder runs without a sound from the beagles, the sun was near the horizon and Tony and Dad were beginning to run out of gas. "Pup, pup, pup, pup," Tony called, leashing Rip, Susie, and three of Susie's kids from an earlier litter.

"The rabbits are holed up today, Dave," Tony said, his voice muffled by a frost-whitened scarf he had knotted over his nose and mouth. "They're smarter than we are. It's just too cold."

"I think so," Dad said, around the stem of his pipe. "Let's head back to the car. The kid's probably pretty cold, too." Nip was content to follow me, so I didn't put a leash on him.

And then it happened. The kid and the puppy hit a rabbit track. Nip circled frantically, his white-tipped tail drawing ovals in the air. "Ay-yarp, ay-yarp, ay-yarp," he yodeled, as he took off down the hot scent trail.

Nip disappeared into the darkening woods, his high-pitched voice slowly looping around and turning toward us. "By God, he's driving it back to us, Dave," Tony said excitedly. "His first rabbit, and he's turned it!"

I swelled with pride. Nip was a prodigy! Tony and Dad raised their shotguns to port arms. We narrowed our eyes and watched for the rabbit to lope into sight.

But it didn't. Nip's yapping stopped. Minutes passed. No rabbit, no Nip.

"Well, he's lost it or holed it," Dad said. "Let's put the first team on it."

Tony released the adult dogs. Surely two masters and three journeymen would shift that rabbit.

"A-roop, A-roop," bugled Rip as he hit the scent. "Karp, karp, karp," hollered Susie. "Yipe, yipe, yipe, yipe," caroled the journeymen. Off they ran in hot pursuit, but within minutes they, too, were silent.

"It's holed up for sure," Tony said. "Let's round 'em up and head for the barn."

About a hundred yards into the woods we found the beagles running back and forth in confusion. "Here's where the rabbit went," Dad said, pointing to a hole in the ground. "You can see his tracks leading right up to it. He's earned his freedom."

Dad pulled out his compass and pointed out the way back to the car. The sun was half down, and long purple shadows were spreading across the snow as we walked. It was my job to keep track of Nip, but I was so cold I had stopped paying attention. Bringing up the rear, I idly counted the dogs. Rip, Susie, Max, Whitey, Lady—where was Nip? "Dad," I yelled, "Nip isn't here!"

"Oh, great," Dad said. "He picked a fine time to run off." Dad started whistling. "Here, pup, pup, pup, pup," Tony called.

"Maybe he's back at the hole," Tony said. Back we went, but Nip wasn't there. Cold and scared, I bent down by the hole to tuck my pant legs into my galoshes.

"Ay-yarp, ay-yarp," squealed Nip, but faintly, as if at a great distance. Tony and Dad cupped their ears. "Ay-yarp," came Nip's voice—from the hole in the ground.

Tony leaned down and listened intently. "Sweet Jesus, the little bugger's down there with the rabbit! He's probably stuck!" We called and called. It was almost dark. "Ay-yarp," cried Nip from the hole, but fainter now. It was really getting cold. "We'll have to dig him out before he freezes to death," Dad said.

It didn't take Dad and Tony long to make decisions. "Davy, you stay here in case he comes out," Dad said. "Tony and I will go home and get picks and shovels. If you get too cold, walk to the farm down the road. C'mon, dogs."

The loneliest thing I ever saw was the single taillight of Tony's Dodge as it winked out of sight through the trees. The loneliest thing I ever heard was the ear-ringing silence of those cold dark woods.

I was too young to have a watch, but a lot of hard, cold time passed as I sat alone by the hole. I called my little dog, I prayed, I cried, I pounded my mittened hands on the frozen ground. He wasn't baying anymore. I didn't want to imagine him down there in the darkness.

Then I heard engines. Headlamps jolted down the road, casting crazy moving shadows in the woods. The engines stopped and I heard voices. I saw a half-dozen lights swinging through the trees, coming slowly closer. Who were all these people? I hollered so they could find me.

Dad was the first to get there, carrying a Coleman lantern and calling "Davy!" Tony was next, leading four other men with lanterns, picks, mattocks, spades, and pry bars.

"This is Dave's boy," Tony said, introducing me. "He's lost his dog."

"Don't worry, kid, we'll get him out of there," said one of the strangers, a short, wiry French-looking man with a mustache. "Charlie, you start here with the pick, and we'll see which way the hole goes. But dig easy! Let's find some branches to hang the lanterns on. Giddown, dog!"

Dog?

It was Nip—wet, dirty, bloody Nip.

In cold weather, cottontails hole up in old woodchuck burrows, and woodchuck burrows have several exits. Down in the burrow and unable to turn around, Nip had dug his way through its passages until he found one of those back doors. It had taken him more than two hours to do it.

"Well, I'll be damned," Dad said.

Nip was exhausted, but he still had a lick for me. Somehow it wasn't cold anymore, so I took off my parka, wrapped Nip in it, and carried him out of the woods.

It was a happy little procession that headed back to our house, Tony's car first, followed by an orange Manitowoc County pickup truck and our Studebaker station wagon. As I burst through the front door, I could smell chili and a big pot of coffee perking on the stove. Mom had built a fire in the fireplace, and seven bowls were set at the dining room table.

There were introductions, and a lot of talk. The French-looking man was Tony's brother-in-law, who worked for the highway department. He had loaded the truck with tools and picked up Charlie, who worked with him. The two other men were from the shipyard, where Dad worked. A couple of phone calls had rounded them up.

It didn't take long for six men and a boy to finish a gallon of chili and a quart or two of coffee. Dad raised his cup in a kind of toast.

"This wasn't much of a New Year's Eve for you guys," he said. "Haven't got a drink in the house, but I thank you."

"Hell," said Charlie. "It was just a little walk in the woods. Could have been my dog out there."

When everyone had left, Dad lit his pipe and smiled at me across the table. "Well," he said, "this is what it's like to have friends."

In our family, we used to sit up until midnight on New Year's Eve, and when Guy Lombardo played "Auld Lang Syne" on the radio we would blow our duck calls and polish off some Canada Dry. I didn't wait for midnight that night. Up in my cold, dark bedroom, Nip's tail was thumping on the comforter.

The Century Run

*I*n my dream I was in a belfry. The bell was ringing, and from the bottom of a long ladder, someone was shouting my name.

Then I woke up. My windup alarm clock was clattering and Dad was calling me from the foot of the stairs.

I opened my eyes and shut the alarm off. It was three thirty in the morning. I put on jeans and a wool shirt, laced up my boots, hung binoculars around my neck, and stuffed my copy of *A Field Guide to the Birds* into a back pocket. It was a Saturday in early May 1954, I was eleven years old, and Dad and I were going to win the Bird Breakfast birding contest.

I'm not sure when Manitowoc's annual Bird Breakfast got started, but in the early fifties it was a minor cultural institution, sponsored by Saint Paul's Methodist Church. For a couple of years it was held at our house just outside the city limits. I don't know why we were chosen to host the event, but I suppose it was because we belonged to the church and had two bathrooms.

The procedure was to arrive at dawn, eat an outdoor breakfast cooked on a Coleman stove, and then go birding. The competitors listed the species they saw, and those who had the most by noon won modest prizes. Scoring was on the honor system, so beginning birders who said they saw rarities like fulvous tree ducks or painted buntings got to count them. Some participants did not go birding at all, but instead hung around Dad and his big cast-iron skillet, eating bacon and eggs and drinking coffee. "My God, Dave, that makes three eggs I've had," a man would say, and Dad would reply, "Five, but who's counting?"

This year, though, Dad was leaving the cooking to Mom. This year, I was old enough to do some fairly serious birding. Dad and I were going to skip breakfast, start out in total darkness, drive briskly from one hot spot to another, and rack up sixty or seventy species. This year, we were going to win.

Mom, Dad, and I had no particular interest in birds until we moved to Manitowoc. But when we bought our house on River Road, we acquired Merle Pickett and Lillian Marsh as neighbors, and they were master birders—experts, sharks. They knew habitats, field marks, and songs and shared their knowledge with everyone. Under their guidance we became birders as well. Not masters, of course, but studious apprentices. And now, with three years of bird-chasing under our belts, Dad and I hoped to be contenders for the father-and-son title.

Down in the kitchen, Dad poured me a half cup of coffee and slapped butter on toast. "Eat quick, and let's get going," he said. "We've got a lot of miles to cover."

Dad planned our day as we finished our coffee. "First stop is the thrush woods," he said. "We should get two or three thrushes and an owl, if we're lucky. Then we'll drive out to Collins for puddle ducks and shorebirds. After that we'll come back here and check out Rahrs' farm. Then the cemetery, Lincoln Park, and the Little Manitowoc, if we can squeeze it all in."

Our beagles, Nip and Rip, yawned and stretched and kept an eye on us. They knew something was up and wanted to be included. Dad reached down and patted Rip's head. "No, we aren't going rabbit hunting and you aren't coming along," he said. "But don't feel bad, boys—in a couple of hours there'll be a hundred people here, and all the leftovers you can eat."

Outside, we paused for a moment in front of the garage. The moon was down, it was pitch dark, and there was a gentle breeze out of the south. From the black sky overhead we heard the faint chipping calls of migrating songbirds. We weren't skillful enough to identify them, but birds were clearly on the move.

Dad raised the garage door. It made its usual screech and was answered by the rasping crow of a cock pheasant somewhere down in the wooded ravine that ran along the east side of our yard. "How about that!" Dad said. "Species number one and we haven't even started the car. It's a good sign."

On our way to the thrush woods, Dad turned on the overhead light in our Studebaker station wagon. He took a folded bird list from his *Field Guide*. "You can be the accountant today," he said, handing me the list. I ran the point of my pencil past the loons and ducks and geese until I came to ring-necked pheasant and made a check. "That's one," I said.

The thrush woods was our name for a woodlot about ten miles west of town. It was split down the middle by a gravel road and we stopped partway through. Dad lowered the Studie's tailgate and we sat on it while he poured some coffee from the thermos and lit his pipe. We waited through five minutes of unbroken silence.

"Come on, owls," Dad whispered. He tapped his pipe on his palm, dislodging a small shower of glowing red embers onto the gravel. Then, at a considerable distance, we heard the first owl of the morning. "Hoo, hoo-hoo, hoo, hoo," it said, in a five-note pattern I had heard once before. Dad struck a match so I could see the list, and I checked off the great horned owl. "That's two," Dad said. "Heard birds count, if you're really sure what they are."

There was a hint of gray in the east. Dad cupped his hands around his mouth. "I wonder if this will produce anything," he said. "I've never tried it, but it's supposed to work." He hooted eight times in a jazzy rhythm.

There was an immediate, loud reply from a tree almost overhead: "Hoo, Hoo Hoo-Hoo, Hoo, Hoo, Hoo Hoo-aw!"

We tried to spot the owl, but it was too dark. "You try it, Davy," Dad said. I hooted, and got a similar answer. The owl was still invisible. "Anyway, it's a barred owl," Dad said. I checked it off. So far we had three species without seeing a thing.

Dad and I sat on the tailgate for another ten minutes, drinking coffee and listening. The thrushes started in shortly after the owls knocked off, and for a while we heard a veery and a wood thrush singing simultaneously on opposite sides of the road.

"Some day," Dad said, "you'll be reading a book and you'll come across the word 'ethereal.' It means heavenly, and it's the only word that describes what we're hearing right now." I glanced up at Dad; I had never heard him say anything like that.

He looked at me and winked. "Well, it describes Audrey Hepburn, too," he said. "She's pretty ethereal."

By this time it was light enough to walk into the woods. We saw hermit and olive-backed thrushes, a brown thrasher, a flicker, and a yellow-bellied sapsucker. Birds were singing all around us. Dad peered through the underbrush. "There's a fallen log over there—let's

84

sit on it for a minute and listen." But when we got close to the log, it seemed to blow up. There was a thunder of wings and a shower of leaves as a large bird rocketed into the air and disappeared.

"Grouse," Dad said. "We must have jumped him off his drumming log." We headed back to the car. On the way we passed through a small clearing, and I flushed a chubby, long-billed bird that ran erratically ahead of us and then twittered into the air. "Woodcock," Dad said.

Back at the car, Dad looked at his watch. "Five thirty. We've got to hit the road for Collins. The sun will be up soon."

I took a last look around. On a lower branch of a big oak I saw a small, white-bellied bird with an eye ring and a long tail. Dad saw it too, studied it with his binoculars, and flipped through his *Field Guide*. "Blue-gray gnatcatcher," he said. "Page one sixty-three."

On the way to Collins Marsh, I checked off the birds we had seen or heard at the thrush woods; we were up to thirteen.

The marsh was a low-lying area along the Manitowoc River. In wet years, it offered a stopping place for migrating ducks and shore-birds. Dad turned down a side road and stopped beside a flooded cornfield that was covered with ducks. He started identifying them and pointing them out to me as I made checks on our list. We saw nine species of ducks, a horned grebe, a hooded merganser, a marsh hawk tilting low over the field, Forster's and black terns, an eastern kingbird, and a yellow warbler. Through the shimmer and glare we thought we could see shorebirds on the far side of the cornfield, but they were too far away to identify with our seven-power binoculars.

"Shoot!" Dad said. "I was counting on getting some shorebirds at this spot. We could walk out there, but there's no cover and we'd just scare them away." I counted up my check marks. "That makes twenty-nine," I said.

Out on the highway, Dad gunned the Studie up through the

gears and leveled off at about fifty. Then I saw some puddles in a grassy field just ahead. Dozens of small, long-legged birds were wading in the puddles.

"Shorebirds!" I yelled, and Dad stamped on the brakes. From behind us came the squeal of tires from a much larger car. It slid to a stop a few feet from our bumper. I looked back and saw the toothy grille of a Nash Ambassador. The car was painted an ominous black and white; it was a state trooper. "Oh, Lord," Dad said, and pulled over onto the shoulder.

The trooper got out of his cruiser, straightened his flat-brimmed campaign hat, and walked slowly up to Dad's side of the car, carrying a leather citation book.

"Why did you stop so short?" the trooper asked. "It's lucky I was paying attention or I would have run you over!"

The trooper had probably been following us too closely, but Dad decided not to mention it. "Well, Officer, we saw those birds over there," he said, pointing. The trooper looked over the top of our car at the puddles.

"So what?" he said.

Dad smiled ingratiatingly. "We're in a contest—a birdwatching contest."

"I never heard of a birdwatching contest," the trooper said. "Who's putting it on?"

"Saint Paul's Methodist in Manitowoc," Dad replied.

"Oh," said the trooper. He didn't seem impressed. He was a big, beefy blond fellow, probably a Lutheran or Dutch Reformed. "So what kind of birds do you see over there?" he asked. He was checking on us.

"Let me look," Dad said, lifting his binoculars. "Well, right in front of us is a Wilson's snipe, and behind him is a flock of dunlins—the little guys with the black bellies—and then just to the left is a semipalmated plover and a pectoral sandpiper. Then there's a solitary sandpiper, and behind it is a little flock of yellowlegs."

Dad rattled on nervously. "Actually there are two kinds of yellow-legs, greater and lesser, but I can't tell which they are at this distance. I think that's pretty much all—except, wait—yes, those little reddish birds drilling in the mud are dowitchers. There's two kinds of them, too—long-billed and short-billed, but they are really hard to tell apart if you can't hear them call . . ."

"OK, OK, I believe you," the trooper said, smiling now. "Tell you what—I was all set to write you a ticket. But you two have made my day. I can't wait for the shift change, so I can tell the other guys about your short-legged doohickeys," he said. "In the meantime, keep an eye on your mirror—somebody might be gaining on you."

Dad lit his pipe as the trooper drove off. "Were you marking those birds down as I was calling them off?" he asked, all business again. "We've got a fifty-fifty chance of being right on the yellowlegs and dowitchers. Mark down one of each." I counted them up. "That makes thirty-six," I said.

On the way home, we looked in all directions at once. The sun was well above the horizon, and we picked up eight more species flying or perched near the road: a turkey vulture, a red-tailed hawk, a chimney swift, numerous crows and starlings, an eastern meadow-lark, a sparrow hawk, and a goldfinch. I added the checks as we pulled up the driveway—the total was now forty-four.

As Dad eased the Studie into the maze of parked cars on our lawn, I spotted Nip and Rip working the crowd of breakfast eaters, polishing off bacon crumbs, cold eggs, and sausage scraps, their white-tipped tails waving. People were lining up to feed them. "I hope they don't get too many eggs," Dad said. "The last thing we need is gassy beagles."

We walked around the house to check out the backyard and the bird feeders and picked up seven more species: a robin, a chickadee, a mourning dove, a downy woodpecker, a white-breasted nuthatch, a palm warbler, and a house wren. I added up the checks again. "Fifty-one," I said. "Halfway there," Dad muttered.

The next stop was Rahrs' farm, across the road from our house. We walked down the long driveway and saw fifteen more species—a great blue heron, a killdeer, a phoebe, a blue jay, three kinds of swallows, a catbird, a cardinal, chipping and song sparrows, red-winged blackbirds, a grackle, a cowbird, and a rock dove. I checked them off. "That makes sixty-six," Dad said. "Two-thirds of the way there."

"Two-thirds of the way where?" I asked. "To the century run," Dad said. "That's what you call it when you get a hundred species in a day. I never thought we could do it, but now we have a chance to make the century run by noon. We've got almost three hours to pick up another thirty-four birds. And we haven't even been to a good warbler spot yet. Let's get going!"

Now that we had a goal to shoot for, our birding took on a fresh intensity. The nearest good warbler spot was Evergreen Cemetery, on the outskirts of Manitowoc about a mile away. Dad let the Studie coast to a stop at the edge of the cemetery, which was bounded on the west by a stand of box elder trees and honeysuckle bushes that attracted migrating warblers every year. As we got out of the car, we could see small birds flitting from branch to branch, never spending more than a few seconds in one place. Warblers were there in droves.

But the mild weather that had pushed the warblers north had also sped up the growth of leaves. The box elders already had leaves the size of squirrels' ears, and the honeysuckles were partially leafed out, making the birds hard to see. We spotted a chestnut-sided and a magnolia, but the rest of the warblers were hidden by foliage.

Dad put his pipe in his mouth and blew through it before filling it. "Drat," he said, "it's plugged up." He blew through it again, but the shred of tobacco stayed put. He pursed his lips and sucked on the end of the stem, and the pipe made a kissing sound ending in a smack. He sucked again and made another smack. I looked back at the honeysuckles and saw a half-dozen myrtle warblers flutter to the outside edge of the bushes, followed by a Cape May and a Blackburnian.

"Do that again, Dad!" I exclaimed. "It's attracting them!" In about a hundred yards of walking and smacking, we saw six more species of warblers—bay-breasted, blackpoll, black and white, redstart, a very early Canada, and a Wilson's—plus a rose-breasted grosbeak and a Baltimore oriole, all brought out of the shrubbery by Dad's pipe.

"The next time I buy a pipe and your mother complains, I'll tell her it's a bird call," Dad said. "That makes seventy-nine—we're getting close. Let's go to the park."

Lincoln Park was on the east side of Manitowoc near the lakeshore. In its center was a stand of big oaks and pines crisscrossed with cinder paths. We walked fast, looking at our watches every couple of minutes, and saw eight new species: a pewee, a great crested flycatcher, three kinds of vireos, a red-breasted nuthatch, a ruby-crowned kinglet, and a common yellowthroat. We circled back to the car. Suddenly Dad stopped in midstride and raised his binoculars.

"On the trunk of that big white pine," he said. "See it? A little greenish bird, no wing bars. I think it's an orange-crowned warbler, but I can't be sure. Oh hell, it flew."

"Should I count it?" I asked. "No," Dad said. "I'm not really sure what it was. Let's save it for an emergency."

"Well, that makes eighty-seven," I said, "not counting the little green bird."

Our last stop was an estuary where the Little Manitowoc River flowed into Lake Michigan. It was alive with waterfowl; the problem was finding birds we had not already seen. We managed to sort out twelve new species—red-breasted and common mergansers, ring-billed and herring gulls, blue-winged and green-winged teal, a pied-billed grebe, a coot, a Canada goose, and a common goldeneye, plus a Caspian tern and a kingfisher.

I totaled my check marks, counting under my breath from the top of the list. "Ninety-nine, one hundred!" I yelled. "We did it. The century run!"

Dad looked at me with a broad grin. He was not a demonstrative man, but he grabbed me in a bear hug, and then quickly let go when our binoculars ground together. Dad looked at his watch. "A hundred species with forty minutes to spare—let's head for the barn," he said.

We were a couple of happy birders as we drove out River Road to our house. A cold east wind had begun to blow off the lake, and the crowd had thinned a bit when we got home at twenty to twelve. I headed up to my bedroom to get my jacket, and as I put it on I realized I still had the bird list in my shirt pocket. I sat down at my desk, picked up a pencil, and quickly recounted my check marks, subtotaling at the bottom of each page.

I added up the column of figures. The total was ninety-nine. Fear clutched at my heart. I counted and added again. The total was still ninety-nine. It was ten minutes to twelve. My brain began to churn. Of all the birds we had not seen, which one could we find in the next ten minutes?

I glanced over at a group of bird pictures that Mom had hung on my bedroom wall. At the bottom was a woodcut of a sparrow bathing in a puddle, with a little poem:

> The muddy sparrow,
> Mean and small,
> I like by far
> The best of all.

House sparrow! I looked at the checklist. I had not marked the house sparrow. Of course, we had seen house sparrows that morning; they were everywhere, like avian wallpaper. But we had not specifically identified one.

I ran outside and found Dad. "I miscounted," I said. "We've only got ninety-nine. We have to find something right away, or otherwise count that little green bird from Lincoln Park."

"It's tempting," Dad said, "but it would be cheating."

Then I remembered something I had read about horses and house sparrows: Horses eat oats, and house sparrows feed on the undigested oats in horse manure. I had no idea where to find a horse, but there were cows aplenty right across the road. They would have to do.

"Come on!" I shouted, and started down the steep path from our yard to the farm driveway. We squeezed through the big wooden gate and ran out into the pasture. Not fifty feet away was a pile of cow manure, and perched on it was a male house sparrow picking at seeds, his feathers ruffled in the wind. We looked at him through our binoculars, to be sure, and we looked at our watches—11:58. I made the hundredth check on the list. We had done the century run in eight hours.

Dad took his pipe from his pocket and tapped the bowl on his palm.

"Good old Wisconsin," he said. "There's always some cow shit around when you need it."

Author's Note: Birders who wonder about the names of some of the species mentioned in this story should be aware that over the years, the names of many birds have been changed to confuse the innocent. In 1954 we were using the second edition of Roger Tory Peterson's *Field Guide to the Birds,* and I have adhered to the names in use back then. In the meantime, for example, the fulvous tree duck has become the fulvous whistling duck, the olive-backed thrush has become the Swainson's thrush, the marsh hawk has become the northern harrier, the Wilson's snipe has become the common snipe, and the sparrow hawk has become the kestrel.

Sacrificing Sweet Sixteen

*O*ut in the woods, a bird hunter lives in the past, the present, and the future at the same time. In the thick of a cover, he lives for the moment. But when he stops for a breather, he thinks of old times and old dogs and looks forward to puppies and seasons to come. And when he has a minute to dream, he dreams of shotguns, because he always could use a better one.

Back in the late 1940s, my dad dreamed of a Sweet Sixteen, the sixteen-gauge version of John Browning's venerable semiautomatic shotgun.

What Dad saw in the Sweet Sixteen was hard to understand. He was used to side-by-sides. As a boy, he learned to shoot with an old Baker twelve-gauge that his father, a county sheriff at the time, had taken away from a man who had shot someone with it. The Baker's barrels had no choke whatsoever, and it was a bird killer as lithe and pitiless as a goshawk. By the late twenties, though, when Dad was in his teens, the Baker had shot loose. Grandpa gave Dad a D. M. Lefever to take its place.

Dad and the Lefever hunted together through the Depression years. Then came 1941, and hunting was largely canceled for the duration. But when the war was over and things had settled down, Dad scraped together enough money to buy a Sweet Sixteen, and the Lefever was moved to the back of the gun rack.

I suppose Dad loved his Sweet Sixteen because it was the first new gun he had ever owned and the first he had ever bought with his own money. And after we moved to Wisconsin, it didn't take long for Dad and the Sweet Sixteen to become a team.

Sunday afternoons in October and November were grouse-hunting time for Dad, and his posthunt rituals are among my fondest memories of him. First, there would be a heavy clumping on the back porch as he kicked the clay out of the cleats on his boot soles. I would run to meet him in the back hall. He'd stand the cased Sweet Sixteen against the wall behind the door and show me the grouse. There always seemed to be two.

He would put the birds in a grocery bag and tuck them in the icebox to cool, so they would be easier to skin and dress. After supper he would clean the grouse on the back porch, carefully fanning out the tail feathers so I could add them to my collection. Then he'd take the Sixteen down to the basement workshop, put a strip of old carpet on the workbench, carefully disassemble the gun, and clean it.

The smells of those grouse-hunting Sunday nights were as memorable as the sights. There would be the mingled scents of muck, sweetfern, and juniper on Dad's boots, the aroma of his pipe tobacco—Walnut if he had some extra money, Kentucky Club if he didn't—the supper smell of Swiss steak and stewed tomatoes from the kitchen, and the odor of gunpowder solvent down in the workshop.

Through all this, childhood was waning. Before long a milestone was reached: I turned twelve and was judged reliable enough to start hunting.

A "first" is always memorable: first kiss, first car, first punch in the nose, first shotgun. After supper on Christmas Eve 1954, Dad headed down the basement stairs and motioned for me to follow. In the workshop was a cabinet where the Sweet Sixteen, the old Baker, the Lefever, and my Savage single-shot .22 rifle were stored. Dad opened the cabinet and took out a slender wand of a shotgun. He pivoted its top lever, swung the barrels down, and handed it to me.

"There you go," he said. "Take care of it. It's a Fox."

I had heard enough shotgun talk to know that a D-grade Ansley H. Fox twenty-gauge ejector double like this one, with a sweeping flame in its oil-finished walnut and deep engraving on its frame, wasn't just any old bird-banger; it was one of the finest shotguns ever made in the United States. And it lay there in my hands like a steel Stradivarius.

Dad smiled. I babbled. I looked down the Fox's gleaming bores, closed its action, and tentatively raised the little gun to my shoulder. And then I looked into the cabinet and realized that the Sweet Sixteen was gone. Dad had traded it, and God only knows how much cash, for the Fox.

"But what about the Browning?" I asked, pointing to the cabinet.

"Oh," Dad said, "that Browning was just a machine. What you've got there is a gun. And besides, I still have the Lefever, and there's about a hundred years of wear left in it."

Brave talk, intended to make me feel better. But I realized, a little bit then and a lot more later, what Dad had given up. For better or for worse, the Sweet Sixteen had been his dream, and Dad had moved his dream aside for me.

Well, you're probably thinking, big deal. Parents sacrifice for their kids' sakes all the time, and usually the kids aren't even aware of it. But on that evening when I was twelve, I tried to understand; I could see that Dad had given up something he wanted very much so that I could have something even better.

There are a lot of ways to show love: a smile, a touch, an apology, a good meal. But giving by giving up is the truest way.

And if you're wondering, there is an immediate reward: you get to feel like Dad did when he handed me the Fox. That's if you're lucky.

The Fine Art of Forgetting

We all do dumb things.

What matters is what we do afterward.

The temptation to be stupid keeps coming around; eventually most of us learn to resist it about half the time, and that's what's known as growing up.

The trouble is, growing up takes a while. Chances are you'll be a full-fledged adult, and more than likely a parent, before you accomplish it. Then the fun starts. You have to avoid being dumb yourself, to set a good example for your kids. But the hardest part is deciding what to do when your kids do dumb things.

If you have too much to say, they'll quit listening to you. If you don't say enough, they won't learn anything from you. The best you can do is to set some standards for them, be there to help, and then try to keep your mouth shut as your kids learn to deal with the stupidity they inherited from you.

Here's how I found some of that out.

When winter finally let go of our little Wisconsin town in May 1955, Dad brought home a station wagon load of twenty-gauge shells and Blue Rock clay pigeons. Every Saturday afternoon that we weren't fishing, we'd put a box of pigeons and five or six boxes of shells into my old Radio Flyer coaster wagon and haul them to the big field behind our house. Dad would sail the clays out with a hand trap, and I'd bang away at them with the Fox shotgun he'd given me for Christmas.

Dad taught me to raise my right elbow and form the shoulder pocket that God created for shotgun stocks. He taught me to lift the gun gently to my cheek and swing it ahead of the target. In time, I was hitting three targets out of four, some days even more.

Once in a while, Dad would bring his twelve-gauge Lefever out to the big field and execute a few targets. He'd pivot from the knees, shoulder his shotgun with exasperating slowness, and turn those Blue Rocks into little clouds of black dust that would drift away on the breeze.

"Just take your time and don't worry about missing a few," he would say. "What matters is being safe and showing some good manners."

Yeah, yeah—I knew all that. But I was a twelve-year-old grouse hunter who had never killed a grouse. I wanted a bird.

There were plenty of grouse in Manitowoc County that fall, and as we hunted our way through October, Dad was getting one about every third time he pulled a trigger.

But the grouse didn't know how good a shot I was. About half the birds I flushed were either out of range, invisible, or on the wrong side of a tree. The other half I missed. I was nothing for five, then nothing for ten. By the time we got into November, the empty shells in the game pocket of my hunting vest had begun to rattle.

One Saturday morning, as we walked down a trail into a cover we called the Sandhill, I spotted a grouse on the ground ahead of us. I stopped and slowly began to raise my shotgun.

"Don't shoot a sitting bird," Dad said quietly. "You won't enjoy it. Just walk toward him and take your chances when he flies."

I tiptoed down the trail. My heart hammered in my ears. Thirty yards, twenty-five, twenty. The grouse cocked its head and stared at me. It froze. I froze.

"G'wan, shoo!" I said.

The grouse flushed with a roar and flew straight down the trail. I missed twice; the bird topped out over some tall popples, banked hard left, and glided out of sight.

Dad lit his pipe. "That's the way they are sometimes," he said. "Every now and then you'll run across one that sits there like a chicken. And it's no fun shooting chickens."

The Sandhill cover was a low, overgrown dune running north and south with a thick cedar swamp on both sides. The dune was growing up in aspen and spruce and brambles, and it was grouse heaven. The birds roosted in the cedars and came out on the dune to eat buds and bugs and blackberries.

Dad sent me down the middle of the dune and walked parallel to me along the edge of the cedars. We hadn't gone more than a hundred yards when a grouse flushed in front of Dad and cut into the swamp. He fired almost instantly.

"Did you get it?" I yelled.

"I don't think so," Dad hollered back. "Wait there and I'll go look."

It was a cool, windless day with a high, gray sky, so quiet that I could hear the confidential "dee, dee, dee" of the chickadees, and the whirrs of their wingbeats as they danced around in the trees.

Then I saw something move in the top of a big spruce ahead of me. It was a grouse, at least thirty feet off the ground, staring at me nervously as it perched on one of the short upper branches. I raised my gun, then lowered it partway. I looked around to my left, where Dad had disappeared into the cedars. I couldn't see him.

I raised the gun again and pointed its slender barrels at the grouse. OK, I thought, maybe I won't enjoy it but by God I'll have a bird. And I pulled the back trigger. The gun cracked and the spruce needles jumped. The grouse toppled from its perch, dead. It fell a couple of feet through the dense branches and got stuck. I hadn't expected that.

Dad called from a distance. "Did you get it?"

"I'm not sure," I lied.

"Well, I'll be over there in a minute to help you look," Dad said. Good old Dad.

The horror of the situation soaked in. Stupid, greedy me, I had shot a sitting bird, I already regretted it, and now I couldn't even retrieve it. The tree was too big to shake, and too bushy to climb.

Looking around, I saw a piece of dead wood about the size of a baseball bat. I put down my gun, grabbed the stick, and hurled it toward the top of the spruce. It fell short. There was plenty of dead wood around, and I threw one chunk after another, but nothing could dislodge that grouse.

Then I heard Dad's voice behind me.

"Well, I'll be damned," he said, in a conversational tone. "Sometimes that happens. You shoot 'em and they fall right into a tree."

That was the lie I was about to tell him! My face burned. How much had he seen?

Dad struck a match and drew the flame down into a fresh bowl of Walnut. We looked at each other. There was a little smile around the corners of Dad's eyes. He knew! He must have been watching the whole time. And he knew I knew he knew.

"So it goes," Dad said. "We'll never get that bird down. Let's hunt 'em up; maybe we'll find some more."

But we didn't. We hunted out the cover and trudged back to the car. I deserved ten minutes of I-told-you-so, but Dad never said a word. Bless his old heart, not a word. And I never shot another sitting bird.

Dad and I hunted grouse together until 1982. The day at the Sandhill cover was never mentioned, until I brought it up on an October afternoon as we drove home from one of our last hunts. A light rain was falling and red leaves scuttled across the road. I told him the story I've just told you, and I thanked him for being so kind.

"I don't remember that," Dad said. "I don't remember that at all. But if you say so . . ."

I glanced over at him but he was busy filling his pipe.

Dad's gone now, and my wife and I have raised a daughter and a son. You're probably wondering how I dealt with them when they screwed up. But you know, I've been lucky. My kids have never done a single dumb thing. Not that I can remember, anyway.

The Secret Smallmouth Lake

in the U. P.

The story of the secret smallmouth lake in the U.P. began in the White House Lunch on a June noon in the mid-1950s.

The White House Lunch was on the north bank of the river, surrounded by the shipyard and the White House milk condensery. It was small, noisy, hot in all seasons, and incredibly busy when the yard was working three shifts.

The White House always smelled pungently of fried onions and cigarette smoke, which darkened the walls and even the pictures of pretty girls and bird dogs on the calendars. When you walked in, Rich, who owned the place, would point to an empty stool at the counter, yell "hamburgeronion" to the kitchen, and slap down a ruby-red plastic glass of ice water. You didn't want a hamburger-onion? Tough. Hamburgeronions were du jour at the White House.

Trouble was coming, but Dad didn't sense it as he left his sweltering office at the shipyard and headed for lunch at the White House that day. Even the hellish spit, pop, and flash of welding in the yard's fabrication shop didn't seem like a warning.

But when the screen door of the White House banged shut behind him, Dad saw that the only vacant spot at the counter was next to Clifford. That was an omen.

Clifford was a thin, lonely, red-headed welder and a breathless, nonstop talker. He lived to fish, but not at local places like Pigeon Lake or the Coast Guard pier. For Clifford, real fishing didn't start until you were at least a hundred miles away, somewhere north of Highway 64, as far back in the woods as possible, and in the company of a good listener.

Clifford saw Dad, smiled, and patted the empty stool beside him. Knowing that Dad was a bass fisherman, he shifted smoothly from perch, which he had been discussing with a grizzled pipefitter, to smallmouth bass in the North Woods.

"Dammit Dave you know that little smallmouth lake up in Michigan I'm always talking about well I was thinking the other day I said to myself dammit I've got to get Dave Crehore up there because he's the only other guy I know who likes smallmouth and why should I keep it to myself I just got a new tent so why don't we drive up there Friday night and camp out right on the lake we won't need a boat and we can take my car so what do you say?" Clifford said.

Dad loved to talk, but he was careful and thorough and no match for Clifford in words per minute. He thought the proposition over as he began the ritual of filling and lighting his pipe.

"Well . . . ," Dad said, between initial puffs.

"Well that's great dammit y'know I found that lake way back in the woods when I was working for the CCC in 1935 we built a little road to it but nobody's been in there since then dammit Dave you're going to love it I'll pick you up after work Friday jeez I'd better get back to the shop," Clifford said.

Dad worked six or seven days a week when the yard was busy, and he had to take his fishing how and when he could get it. And so it came to pass that on the following Friday afternoon, he sat on the porch with his waders, tackle box, bedroll, frying pan, coffee pot, "6-12" mosquito dope, flashlight, and axe. Atop the pile were aluminum tubes holding his treasured nine-foot Wright & McGill Granger Special fly rod and an equally precious six-foot, five-sided Airex bamboo spinning rod. Canvas bags held a Pflueger Medallist reel for the fly rod and a Bache Brown spinning reel loaded with fifty yards of the latest braided nylon line. What is so rare, he thought, as a day in June on a wilderness bass lake that hasn't been fished since 1935?

But when Clifford pulled up, almost on time, Dad's sunny optimism began to cloud over. For one thing, Clifford's fishing car was remarkably old, a prewar Hudson with faded paint and a rotted muffler.

"By golly Dave you're all ready let's get your stuff in the trunk dammit this is going to be fun careful the door latch on your side doesn't work," Clifford said.

"OK," Dad said.

And off they went, west on Highway 10 to Appleton and New London, north on 45 to Antigo, where they bought Michigan licenses at a bait shop, and on to Land O' Lakes.

It was midnight when they crossed the Michigan line and entered the U.P. Bats and bugs fluttered in the headlight beams as they drove through young plantations of red pine. Then Clifford slowed down.

"Dammit Dave I'm pretty sure we take the next right and go east about five miles or so woops I think that's the road but I'd better drive on and make sure it isn't the next one—no that doesn't look like it I think it really was the first one so I'll turn around and go back," Clifford said.

Clifford turned off the highway onto a narrow gravel road. After they had climbed the first couple of hills, the road turned into a two-rut logging trail. As they ground along in first gear, the ruts narrowed, the grass between them got taller, and the hills got steeper. And the Hudson began to slow down. Finally it stopped altogether halfway up a hill.

"Jeez Dave I wonder what's wrong I sure am glad you brought a flashlight my God the mosquitoes are thick you'll have to hold up the hood for me dammit the accelerator cable is busted no wonder it won't run suffering Christ how are we going to fix it?" Clifford said.

Dad dug his tackle box out of the trunk and found a wire musky leader. With his fishing pliers he cut the leader to size and spliced it to the stub of the broken cable with a pipe cleaner. It worked perfectly.

"Dammit Dave it sure was a good idea to bring an engineer along now listen to her roar the old girl hasn't run this strong in years well let's get going the road to the lake is just over the top of this hill I think we're almost there," Clifford said.

The road to the lake wasn't over that hill or the next one but they finally found it, a faint track leading off to the left, almost invisible in the spill of light from the headlamps.

"Dammit Dave I'm pretty sure this is it let's stick our nose up here and find out jeez it's rough look at that popple right in the middle of the road the bugger must be three inches thick 'course I haven't been down this road in twenty years," Clifford said.

Out came the axe and down went the popple. "Dammit Dave you're a regular Paul Bunyan wow here comes the wind was that lightning off there to the west yup there it goes again well we better get a wiggle on it's only about a mile to the lake," Clifford said.

It was two miles to the lake, two miles of overgrown trail blocked by four more popples that had to be felled and about a dozen smaller oncs that Clifford pushed down with the car and ran over. The branches of the last popple tore off the Hudson's exhaust pipe and left it lying on the trail.

Liberated from its muffler, the Hudson snarled like a P-51. The western sky was livid with lightning, branches of overhanging trees clawed at the car, and a rain of biblical proportions began to fall. The windshield was soon covered with wet leaves and twigs that jammed the feeble wipers.

And then, deliverance. Jolting and bouncing, the Hudson splashed into a small clearing and its lights shone onto open water.

"Sonofagun Dave we finally made it dammit I knew this was the right road well let's get the tent set up before we drown she's a brand-new rubber-covered Canadian army surplus mountain tent guaranteed waterproof I don't suppose you've ever set one of these up 'cause I've never had her out of the bag jeez it's windy dammit there goes the instructions."

With Clifford holding the flashlight, Dad stuck Pole A into Slot B until the reeking, crumbling tent assumed a rough inverted V-shape. Grabbing their bedrolls from the car, they shoehorned themselves into the tent. Exhausted by driving, talking, and watching, Clifford fell asleep instantly, but Dad remained awake to reflect on life's rich tapestry.

First of all, it was obvious to Dad that Canadian soldiers had run small in the '40s, because the tent, advertised as a two-man, was only big enough for a honeymoon couple. Never a touchy-feely type, Dad spent the first half hour trying to edge away from the snoring Clifford, who kept snuggling up like an affectionate golden retriever.

Second, he noted that like most items described as "waterproof," the Canadian mountain tent did a better job of keeping water in than out. Before an hour had passed, the condensed sweat and exhalations of two men began dripping down on him from the tent's roof.

Third, he wondered about the persistent, snuffling, bad-smelling thing that was trying to open the Hudson's trunk and steal the bacon. A skunk? A bear? Or—this was Michigan—a wolverine?

Morning came early. Driven by an overwhelming need to escape Clifford's clutches, brew some coffee, and light his pipe, Dad gave up trying to sleep and crawled out of the tent into the gray-blue light of false dawn.

It wasn't hard to find a little dry birchbark, and within a half hour he had a quart of lake water boiling over a small fire. Sitting on the Hudson's front bumper, Dad sipped a tin cup of gritty camp coffee, sucked down refreshing puffs of Walnut, and watched fanciful towers of ground fog drift across the lake.

The rain had washed the clouds away, and as the eastern sky turned to yellow, Dad could see that the lake was a jewel, about a hundred acres of iron-stained water surrounded by dense stands of cedar. Maybe, just maybe, it will be worth it, he thought, as he put the Granger together, threaded up the line, and tied on a Dr. Henshall bass bug. Maybe a couple of naive wilderness smallmouth would join them for breakfast.

"Old Sam Peabody, Peabody, Peabody," sang the white-throated sparrows as Dad made cast after cast into the beautiful little lake. No bass were forthcoming, but it hardly mattered. The sun and a gentle breeze eased over the eastern horizon together and brushed golden ripples on the water.

Hypnotized by the birdsong, the glittering lake, and the rhythm of casting, Dad hardly noticed the first flash of light from the opposite side of the lake. The second flash, on the periphery of his vision, got his attention, and he stopped fishing to watch for another. In a few minutes there was a third flash. It was the reflection of the rising sun from the windshield of a fast-moving car.

"Clifford," Dad said, as he prodded the tent from the outside, "there's a highway on the other side of this lake."

"I'm up I'm up jeez Dave there can't be because I fished all the way around it in '35 and there wasn't no other road."

"Well," Dad said, "there is now."

After two hours of fishing which yielded one angry, stunted rock bass, Dad and Clifford packed up and headed for home. They stopped for gas at a station in Watersmeet, and while Clifford took his turn in the men's room, Dad asked an elderly mechanic for a little Upper Peninsula lore.

"About five miles east and two miles north there's a lake back in the woods that used to have real good smallmouth fishing. Know anything about it?"

"Oh God, don't bother going over there," said the old-timer. "It was our secret bass lake in the '20s—took half a day to walk back into it. But the government cut a trail to the south side in '35, and those CCC boys about fished her out. Then after the war when the new highway got built along the north shore, she just went to hell. Ain't good for nothing but rock bass now."

The following Monday noon, as Dad lingered over his hamburgeronion at the counter of the White House, he heard a familiar rapid-fire voice from a booth in the back. Clifford had found another victim.

"Dammit Fred I just got back from the best doggone weekend of fishing I ever had you know Dave Crehore well he and I drove up to Michigan to a little bass lake I found when I was working for the government by golly we had to chop our way in but we caught smallmouth like hell wouldn't have it say you know there's a little spring pond not too far from there and nobody's been to it in years it's just full of brook trout and I know you're crazy about them hey let's drive up there this weekend I got a brand new tent just used once and we can take my car I'm telling you you're gonna love it what do you say?"

"Well . . . ," Fred said, as he tapped a Pall Mall on the side of his Zippo . . .

The Butternut Buck

When I was a boy in the 1950s, my Grandpa Crehore gave me three gifts that weren't toys or books: a faded photograph of himself carrying a whitetail buck, the buck's mounted antlers, and a story that went with them. The photo and the old rack are going to stay in the family, but here's the story.

Grandpa and his friend Wally crested a cutover hill and stopped for a rest, their breath shooting out in clouds of steam. It had snowed about an inch that morning, and the afternoon was cold, crisp, and windless.

The tracks of a rutting buck they had jumped an hour earlier cut diagonally down the slope before them and disappeared into a cedar swamp.

"We could spend a week in that swamp and never see him, George," Wally said. "I'll bet he's gonna circle around in the swamp and try to sneak back out to his lady friend. There's a couple hours of good daylight left. Why don't I go down to where his tracks head into the swamp, and you go over about a hundred yards west, and we'll just wait and see what happens."

"Sounds good to me, Wally," Grandpa said. Grandpa trudged off downhill, then turned and took a stand on the edge of the swamp where he could see into the cedars.

A half hour passed. It got colder. A chickadee hung upside down from a branch a foot from Grandpa's rifle barrel, sang a quiet "dee, dee, dee," and flew off.

Suddenly, a stone's throw back in the swamp, something moved. Was it another chickadee, a jaybird, or the buck? Grandpa froze and stared. "I figured there was a fifty-fifty chance the buck was there," he said later. "I couldn't see him. All I could do was hold still and wait him out."

A hundred rapid heartbeats went by. Finally, the buck took a cautious step forward and Grandpa saw its outline against the green and brown background of the swamp. He thumbed back the hammer of his Winchester 94 and eased the little rifle to his shoulder. The buck took another step and turned, looking directly at him. Grandpa lined up the sights on a spot behind the buck's front leg and fired.

The .30-30 went off with a crack that sent snow cascading from nearby cedar branches and made Grandpa's ears ring. Obscured by powder smoke and the falling snow, the buck seemed to disappear. Grandpa plunged ahead a few steps, looked again, and saw that the buck had fallen in its tracks. He could hear Wally yelling off in the distance. He levered a fresh cartridge into the chamber and walked the remaining thirty yards or so, ready for a second shot.

But no more shooting was necessary. The buck lay motionless, sprawled in the snow. Grandpa opened the action of his rifle and leaned it against a tree. Grabbing the buck by its forelegs, he dragged it a few feet, turned it belly side up, and rested its shoulders against a massive old white pine stump. He admired its eight-point rack for a moment, then drew his hunting knife from its sheath and prepared to make the initial cut.

And that's when all hell broke loose.

My paternal grandfather, George J. Crehore, was born in Sheffield Township, Ohio, in 1883. In 1902 he started to learn the pipefitting trade at a shipyard in Lorain, Ohio. But early in 1908 the economic depression of those years hit the shipyard, and at twenty-five Grandpa found himself without a job. He shipped out as a deckhand on a lake freighter, but the lake trade was pretty slow as well. In midsummer, the freighter laid up for the season in Manitowoc, and Grandpa was out of work for the second time in a year. Luckily, the Manitowoc shipyard needed a pipe fitter, and Grandpa settled into a good job that lasted until 1913, when he returned to Ohio and went into business for himself.

The Manitowoc years were eventful for Grandpa. He mastered his trade. He got married. George and Charlie, the first of his five children, were born. He bought a house on Western Avenue. He formed a lifetime friendship with Wally, another shipyard worker. And he took up deer hunting.

Actually, the deer hunting was Wally's idea. He hunted in Ashland County, taking the old Wisconsin Central railroad from Manitowoc to Spencer, and then north to Medford, Prentice, Park Falls, and Butternut. At Butternut, a farmer with a wagon and team would meet Wally and his friends at the station and haul them about fifteen miles to a dilapidated pioneer log cabin in the woods. Since

Grandpa was from northern Ohio, where deer were only a memory at the time, Wally convinced him that his life would be incomplete until he went deer hunting "up north by Butternut."

And so the late fall of 1909 found Grandpa at the deer camp with Wally. The season was twenty days long that year, from November 11th through the 30th. About 103,000 hunters bought one-dollar licenses that allowed them to take "any one deer" in the thirty-one northern counties that were open for deer hunting; south of a line from Peshtigo to Prairie du Chien, deer were rare and the season was closed. There was no deer registration back then, so there's no record of the total kill, but rail shipments of deer that season totaled 3,985—slim pickings.

About noon on November 12, their first day of hunting, Grandpa and Wally caught a doe and a good-sized antlered buck in the act of creating more deer. The doe scented them and bolted into the woods. The buck turned and glared.

"He was only about fifty yards away," Grandpa said later, "but we were too surprised to shoot. I imagine he was good and mad at us. And then he took off and we tracked him into the cedar swamp."

"I shot him," Grandpa said, "and he went down in a heap, but just when I touched the knife to him, all hell broke loose!"

The buck thrashed back and forth and struggled to its feet. Grandpa staggered and fell backward, his knife flying off into the snow. The buck swapped ends, lowered its head, and stabbed its antlers at Grandpa's midsection, worrying him like a terrier with a rat. Weaponless and flat on his back, Grandpa grabbed the buck's rack in self-defense, and was amazed to find that the deer could lift him up from the waist and slam him back down again. One of the larger tines of the buck's antlers slid into the fly of Grandpa's woolen "cruiser" pants and ripped it open, showering buttons.

Grandpa heard Wally yelling again, much closer, and then there was a deafening roar as Wally's .30-40 Krag went off at point-blank range. The buck leapt straight up and fell kicking at Grandpa's side. In seconds, it was dead.

It got quiet in the woods again.

"My God, George, are you all right?" Wally asked, his voice trembling.

"My God, yourself," said Grandpa, sitting up. "You coulda killed me!"

"George, he was going to open you up like a melon!" Wally said.

"Don't get personal," Grandpa said.

The two men turned the deer over. The Krag's big bullet had hit the deer in the brisket and had left an exit hole the size of a fist. But there was no other bullet wound.

"He went down like a ton of bricks when I shot him," Grandpa said. "I must have hit him somewhere!"

"George, look at this," Wally said. He pointed to where a ragged chunk had been shot out of the buck's left antler about an inch above the skull. "This is fresh," he said. "You knocked him out!"

Grandpa walked out to the edge of the swamp and looked back. "I fired from here, and I held right behind his leg. There's no way I could miss by two feet at this range." And then Grandpa noticed a broken cedar branch dangling down about ten feet from where he had been standing. With his right eye focused on the rifle's front sight, he hadn't seen the branch. It had deflected his .30-30 bullet up and to the right, blasting a piece out of the buck's antler and knocking him cold.

"Nice deer you got there, Wally," Grandpa said.

"Hell, it's your deer, George," Wally said. "You put him down for a ten-count, and then you rassled with him for a while—he's yours."

"OK," Grandpa said. "And since you saved me from a fate worse'n death, I'll carry him the first hundred yards."

Back at the cabin, Wally got out his Kodak and snapped a picture of Grandpa with the Butternut Buck on his shoulders. By that time, the other hunters in the party had hung a half-dozen deer on the buck pole, and two days later the whole gang was on the train back to Manitowoc, their deer stowed away in the unheated baggage car.

The train pulled into Manitowoc at about ten thirty at night. The deer were unloaded. The hunters checked their rifles and duffles with the stationmaster, lifted the deer to their shoulders, said their good-byes, and headed home down the dimly lighted streets. None of them had cars; the Ford Model T had been introduced only the previous year.

Grandpa said the dressed weight of the Butternut Buck increased about ten pounds a block as he plodded home with it, across the Tenth Street bridge, west on Franklin, then up Water and Clark Streets to Western Avenue. Grandpa wasn't much of a drinker, but he was disappointed when no one came out of the tavern at Tenth and Franklin to admire his deer.

The only people he met were two elderly German-speaking ladies on their way home from a sheepshead game, and they seemed to be scared of him. But as Grandpa said, how would you like to meet a 250-pound man with a six-day beard, wearing a bloody Mackinaw and dirty woolen pants that wouldn't stay buttoned, carrying a deer down *your* street?

The ladies crossed the snowbank into the street to let Grandpa pass.

"*Waltrud, mein Gott, wer ist das?*" one of them said. (Waltrud, my God, who is that?)

"*Ich weiss nicht,*" said the other. "*Ein Jager, ein schmutziger Jager!*" (I don't know. A hunter, a filthy hunter!)

When Grandpa finally got the deer onto his front porch, Grandma met him at the door and kissed him. Someone, at last, appreciated the Butternut Buck. He dumped the deer on the porch floor and straightened up, groaning.

"George, for heaven's sake, button up your pants," Grandma said.

"I can't, Anna," Grandpa said, and told her the story.

Grandma didn't know whether to laugh or scold, so she laughed. "You had him by the horns, and Wally shot him right on top of you . . . heavenly days!"

She smiled at Grandpa. "I hope you thanked Wally. He did you a real favor."

"Yes, I thanked him," Grandpa said. "Several times. And you'd better thank him, too. You're the one that wants a big family."

The Celebrated Water Witch

of Door County

$\mathcal{G}$reat Godamighty," Clifford said, in a tense whisper.

"Great Godamighty there's water right under me here I can feel it dammit look at the willow rod go down!"

Dad tapped the cold ashes out of his pipe into the palm of his hand. "You think you've got it this time?" he asked.

"Oh yeah," Clifford said, raptly. "Oh yeah, here it is!"

Dad turned away to hide a smile. He didn't have much faith in dowsing, the ancient, magical art of finding underground water with a willow stick. But he did appreciate peculiarity, and on this quiet Door County morning in the summer of 1956, his friend Clifford was exhibiting peculiarity unusual even for him. Dad figured it wouldn't do to break the spell.

Clifford stood bolt upright, rigid and trembling with a wide-eyed smile on his face. Clearly he believed he was having a mystical experience of some kind, and sure enough, his Y-shaped, willow dowsing rod was trembling and pointing down.

Suddenly he relaxed. The connection with the infinite had apparently been broken. Clifford turned to Dad with a delighted grin.

"By God Dave this dowsing stick works just like Old Lady Grun said it would—have faith and you can find water anywhere she said and dammit there it is." With the heel of his boot, he kicked a hole in the sand to mark the spot. Water began obligingly to well up in the hole.

"Hot damn Dave look at that I know a good deal when I see one this rod was the best five bucks I ever spent doggone it I didn't even hafta dig boy you got to get up pretty early in the morning to fool me I'll tell you by God I really think I'm born to this dowsing business dammit the feeling comes right up that stick and into my arms," Clifford said.

Dad sat down on an old oil drum that was part of the flotsam on Clifford's narrow strip of Door County shoreline and refilled his pipe. He struck a match on the drum, lit the pipe, and gently tamped the tobacco with the end of his pocketknife.

Dad had never met Old Lady Grun, but he knew her by reputation. She was Manitowoc's "cat lady," a faded crone of seventy or so who lived alone in a small house on the south side. She made a meager living selling cats, of which there were always a couple of dozen around the place, and an assortment of literature ranging from *Mein Kampf* to *Sunshine and Health,* the forbidden Swedish nudist magazine. She also dabbled in horoscopes and magical items like marked poker decks and homemade dowsing rods. Kids in her neighborhood crossed the street before passing her house.

And now, in the hands of a true believer, Old Lady Grun's dowsing rod had found water on a level beach ten feet from the shoreline of Green Bay, where a child with a tin spade and bucket could have found it with much less trouble. Dad reviewed some sarcastic remarks and rejected them, because, in a way, Clifford's Door County venture was his fault.

Clifford was a welder at the shipyard where Dad worked as a marine engineer. Wiry, nervous, a confirmed bachelor, and a breathless, nonstop talker, Clifford reminded Dad of a fox terrier—a busy, bristly, likeable little man who would grab a new idea, chew on it for a while, and then bury it and sniff around for another. Earlier in the '50s, Clifford had fought the Red Menace with "Tail-Gunner Joe" McCarthy, but when the junior senator from Wisconsin went into a tailspin, Clifford swore off politics and became a devotee of vegetarianism—until he tired of sauerkraut and canned green beans, the principal vegetables served by the diners where he ate most of his meals.

Then someone told him that the smart money was being invested in Door County real estate, and that passion preoccupied him until he bought the dowsing rod. During a lunch break at the shipyard a couple of weeks earlier, when Clifford was still shopping for Door County land, Dad had given him an ad torn from the *Manitowoc Herald-Times*.

"You're always talking about buying some land in Door County, Cliff," Dad said. "Well, here you go— 'Irregular parcel with 200 feet of Green Bay shoreline, highway access, $1,000 or best offer, contact Sligh Realty, Sturgeon Bay.'"

"Jeez thanks Dave," Clifford said. "That's just what I've been looking for and it's really cheap too just five bucks a front foot dammit I'll go up there Saturday and look it over."

The parcel was irregular, all right—200 feet long but only 20 feet from front to back, bounded by the Green Bay shore on one side and a county highway on the other, and covered with stones, sand, little trees, and old gull nests. It didn't take long for the real estate agent to realize that Clifford was about as irregular as the parcel. The following weekend Clifford signed the papers and became a Door County land baron.

"Dammit Dave," Clifford said, as he stuck the dowsing rod in the back pocket of his overalls, "buying this land was just like haggling over an old Ford. Sligh he started out at a thousand and I shook my head and walked away so he came down to nine hundred but I kept walking away and he kept coming down till we finally settled on seven hundred I think I could have got him down to six-fifty but there was only so far I could walk 'cause we drove up there in his car."

"Well," Dad said, "there's water, I guess, but there isn't room to build anything here, y' know—you've only got about a tenth of an acre. Looks like you paid seven hundred bucks for a gull sanctuary."

"I suppose so Dave but dammit the way to get rich up here is to bide your time, so I'll just hang on to this and we'll see what happens," Clifford said.

Dad tamped his pipe again. Like most men his age, he had been tried in the furnace of the Great Depression, which taught him to spend his money on things he had to have right now. If a few dollars were left at the end of the month they were parked in an insured savings account at the First National, where he could get his hands on them, and that was that. In Dad's experience, investment was a confidence game in which people who wore suits took money from people who didn't. He hated to see a friend get involved, especially one as naive as Clifford.

But a more immediate problem awaited Dad later that day when he got home from Door County. The stench that billowed out of the house when he opened the back door told him all he needed to know. Pipe smoking had taken the fine edge off Dad's sense of smell, but the odor of a backed-up septic tank was unmistakable. And right behind the odor came an eruption of profanity. Mom was down in the basement, battling the stink and swearing.

Dad was astounded. In fifteen years of married life he had heard her swear only once before, when she woke up on their first morning in Manitowoc and found a bat clinging to the bedroom wall. But this was a different sort of swearing altogether, continuous, biting, and fluent. He had no idea any woman could swear as well as Mom was swearing now, with a fine rhythm and in complete sentences. Dad kicked off his shoes, put on a pair of five-buckle galoshes, grabbed a mop, and joined her in the basement.

Two hours later, when the worst of the sewage had been bailed out and the windows were open to ventilate the house, Mom explained what had happened.

The fine summer day had fired her with domestic energy. She did two big loads of laundry in the Maytag wringer washer, discharging about a hundred gallons of soapy water down the drain. She waited for the water heater to recover from the strain, did a sinkful of dishes, and washed her hair. She waited again and took a relaxing bath. And then, overwhelmed by all that water in one day, the septic tank backed up, filling the basement to a depth of two or three inches. Feeling a need to do something about the smell, she tried to neutralize it with a full quart of Lysol, creating a sweet-sour bouquet that soaked into the basement floor and lasted for years.

"Charlotte, we have to put in a new septic tank and we might as well replace the well while we're at it," Dad said. "We can't put up with this any longer. We'll just have to take the money out of savings."

The well was in a pit out in the yard. It sucked water from the glacial clay that underlay our property to a depth of about a hundred feet. It produced very hard water very slowly, but at least we knew where it was. The septic tank was a mystery. We believed it to be somewhere northeast of the house, but that was just a guess.

That evening, Dad leafed through the Yellow Pages in search of well drillers and septic tank installers. He found the trades dominated by tribes of closely related Dutchmen. At lunchtime the next day, he started calling them.

The well driller was the first to show up. "Shallow wells in this clay aren't any good," he said. "To get good water you gotta go down through the clay to the limestone, enso? You oughta get good water there. But if you don't, then you gotta go down through the shale to the sandstone. One way or the other, we can get you water here, no trouble. But the important thing is to put the well as far as we can from the septic tank, enso?"

The septic tank man agreed with his cousin the well driller. "We gotta find the old tank before we can do anything," he said. "It looks like your drain goes out by the northeast corner of the house, so we got to dig a pit and find the pipe. Then we can figger out where the tank is. Can't start the well 'til we know."

In a few days the pit was dug. The septic tank man stood in the pit with a compass and straddled the pipe. "OK, she goes due northeast like we thought," he said. "So the tank is on a line someplace between here and the gully over there. Once the well is in I'll dig some holes with the auger until we find the old tank. Then we can pull it out and put a new one in the same hole. 'Course we'll have to put in a new drain field too, enso?"

"Enso," Dad said.

The well driller returned for his second visit the next day. "Now we're getting someplace," he said. "We know the septic tank will be going in over there, more or less, so we can put the new well right here," he said, poking a stake with a red flag on it into the lawn close to the house. "This'll be a good place—it's a long way from the septic tank and my brother won't have no trouble getting the drilling rig in here. He can start next Monday."

On the Sunday morning before the well driller was due, Dad had to work at the shipyard. Mom and I dropped him off on our way to church and arranged to pick him up again about noon.

Clifford was at loose ends that morning. Dad had told him about the well and septic tank projects, so he decided to drive out to our place and see how they were getting along. He opened the front door of the house—we never locked it—and hollered for Dad. Finding no one home but our beagles, he decided to have a look around anyway. He got the dowsing rod from his car and headed for the stake with the red flag on it.

"This must be where they want to put in the well let's just see if those guys have any idea how to find water," he said to himself. Clifford grasped the forked end of the dowsing rod and began to walk slowly in a circle around the stake. Nothing. The rod hung lifeless in his hands. He spiraled out in wider circles. Still nothing.

"Ya ya that's just what I expected there ain't no water here the trouble with them damn Dutchmen is they got a lotta machinery and no inspiration," he muttered.

Clifford started walking toward the deep ravine that ran along the east side of our yard. As he approached the edge the dowsing rod suddenly came alive. First it trembled slightly. Then it began to vibrate visibly, and finally it plunged downward as though it were playing a fish.

"I knew it I knew it I knew it!" Clifford exulted. He laid the rod on the ground to mark the spot, pulled up the stake with the red flag, and drove it into the grass at the new location the dowsing rod had found.

The next morning, Dad got a phone call at his office.

"Mr. Crehore, this is Fred the well driller—Jim's brother," he said. "We got started drilling about an hour ago and I guess we got good news and bad news."

"Better give me the bad news first," Dad said.

"Well, the bad news is that we got to move the drilling rig, and that'll cost an extra fifty bucks, but the good news is that we found the old septic tank. We started drilling and punched right through the top of the damn thing. Can't imagine why that flag was there. Made no sense at all. Anyway, Jim came over and told me where the well's supposed to be. We're movin' the rig right now and we'll get started again this afternoon."

"Fine," Dad said.

At lunch that day, Dad gave Clifford a stern look.

"Were you out at our place Sunday morning?" he asked. "And did you move a stake with a red flag on it?"

"Well dammit Dave as a matter of fact I did I walked around with my willow stick and damn if I didn't find a lot of water over by the gully so I just thought I'd do you a favor and . . ."

It was hard to interrupt Clifford but Dad managed it.

"Well, your favor cost me fifty bucks, Cliff," Dad said. "What you found was the old septic tank."

Clifford pulled his wallet from the pocket of his leather welding apron. "Forty-eight, forty-nine, fifty," he counted. "But dammit Dave the thing was full of water, wasn't it?"

When Dad retired in the summer of 1974 the shipyard gang threw a party for him. Clifford was a prominent guest.

"Dammit Dave now you're footloose you gotta come up to my place in Door County for a weekend sometime and bring the missus it's always so nice and cool up there." Clifford said.

"You mean to tell me you built a house on that little strip of land you bought?" Dad asked.

"No no I got a two-acre lot with lots of trees just north of Ephraim with a little cabin on it I swapped it for my land along the bay," Clifford said.

"But Cliff, that land was worthless," Dad said.

"Well, dammit it was and it wasn't," Clifford said. "You remember all them little trees that was growing on it back in 1956 well they just kept on growing for eighteen years and then Sligh he decided to build a bunch of cottages right across the road from my land on the bay.

"Only trouble was you couldn't see the bay from them cottages because of my trees and the customers said they wouldn't buy unless they could watch the sunset from their front porch so Sligh he come to me and we worked out a little trade and he got my land and I got the Ephraim place," Clifford explained. "Dammit Dave it's just like Old Lady Grun told me, just have faith and things will work out OK, enso?"

"Enso," Dad said.

Lucky Thirteen

$\mathcal{I}$nto each life the thirteenth year must fall.

It's a year of change. At thirteen, kids plunge headfirst into the whirlpool of adolescence and their parents are demoted from demigods to ordinary people. With so much going on, the potential for family melodrama is high.

But in my memory, at least, I got through my thirteenth year in pretty good shape. I don't recall battling my parents very much, or embarrassing them, or being embarrassed by them. Most of my peers shunned the company of their parents at that age, but I don't remember feeling that way. I suppose that was because my parents were capable people who did interesting things.

Mom, for instance, had a B.A. in English literature and took advantage of it, as a teacher and a book reviewer. She was also the only parent I knew of who still practiced the piano at the age of forty-three, working her way through a thick book of Mozart sonatas, pieces that sound angelically simple but are fiendishly difficult to play. Hearing them, you can imagine Mozart dipping his quill pen in the inkwell, scratching down a few bars, playing them on his klavier, and grinning an evil Austrian grin.

Anyway, Mom accepted the challenge. Her struggle with the Mozart sonatas became a kind of wrestling match that went on for years, best two falls out of three, Charlotte vs. Wolfgang the Destroyer. I remember coming home from school one September afternoon and hearing Mom at the piano as she took apart and reassembled the Allegro movement of one of the sonatas, like a mechanic working under the hood of a car. I waited on the porch and listened through the screen door, not wanting to interrupt as she practiced a particularly nasty passage. It involved sweeping arpeggios that required a cross-handed, left over right technique.

Mom sailed into it, full speed ahead, and thundered successfully through the first page or so until she reached the culminating measures, which were like a musical barbed-wire fence. She hesitated for a fraction of a second, glared at her fingers, and strummed the mighty chord, tripping over the final notes. She stopped, rested her hands on the keys, and then started over, half speed at first, and then accelerating as she approached the fence. She stumbled again and slammed the lid down on the keys of the Chickering.

"You bastard!" she exclaimed, as though Mozart were in the room. Out on the porch, I laughed.

Mom spun around on the piano stool, saw me for the first time, and blushed. "I'm sorry, Davy—I lost my temper," she said. "I made a cherry pie for supper. Why don't you cut a piece and make sure it's OK?" And five minutes later she and Mozart were back in the ring.

Who could rebel against a parent as exquisitely human as that?

And who made excellent pies to boot? There are worse things than coming home to Mozart and cherry pie.

Dad loved music, and every now and then he would get out his clarinet and play a few scales. But his job required most of his time.

Dad was a marine surveyor for the American Bureau of Shipping. In shipyard talk, "surveying" is the art and science of inspecting the condition and seaworthiness of a ship, and the bureau was a non-governmental agency that set standards for the repair and construction of ships. In the '50s, the Manitowoc Shipbuilding Company was building one big Great Lakes freighter after another, and it was Dad's job to certify every nut, bolt, weld, and rivet.

One Saturday afternoon in May 1956, I went with Dad to the shipyard and watched while he inspected some welds that joined sheets of steel plating. He examined them inch by inch, and after a half hour or so he found a flaw in a seam that went around a curve. Dad marked the flaw with a fat stick of chalk and called the welding foreman over.

"You'll have to burn this one apart and try it again," Dad said. "When you see pits like that there may be a void underneath."

"Bullshit!" said the foreman. "I had my best man on this and those pits don't mean a thing."

"Maybe not," Dad said, calmly, "but it's got to be done over."

"I'd like to see you do it any better!" the foreman yelled.

Apparently the foreman thought that if he shouted loud enough, Dad would wipe off the chalk mark. I waited to see what would happen next.

Dad spoke even more quietly. "All right," he said, "let me borrow a helmet."

A few feet away lay two similar pieces of steel that had to be welded in the same way, curve and all. Dad put on a welder's helmet and apron, started up the generator, and began to weld. The foreman and I stared at the ground to avoid looking at the blue-white arc. After a couple of minutes Dad shut off the generator and tipped the welding helmet back on his head. He had laid an even, flowing bead around the curve.

"See," Dad said, "you have to time it. If you go too fast you lose your heat and you get those pits."

He removed the helmet and wiped the sweat from his forehead. The foreman was bent over Dad's weld, studying it closely. Then he turned and stood looking away from us for a full minute. When he faced us again he shook his head from side to side and pursed his lips, trying to stifle a smile. Then he reached out and punched Dad gently in the shoulder.

"You son-of-a-gun," he said. "You son-of-a-gun. OK, we'll burn the bad one out and do it over."

Dad smiled. "See you Monday," he said. "C'mon, Davy, it's time for supper."

On the way home, I mulled over what I had seen and heard. I already knew that Dad was a jack-of-all-trades, so the fact that he could operate a welding outfit didn't surprise me. But I wondered why he had kept lowering his voice when the foreman started shouting.

"That guy was way out of line. You should've read him the riot act," I said.

"No," Dad replied. "I've got to work with him every day. Now he knows that I can weld a little, and that I won't back down, and that I won't run to his boss every time there's a problem. My job will be easy from now on."

I had found out a lot that afternoon; Dad's methods were slowly making sense to me, clicking into place in my head. But there was one problem.

"Dad?" I said, as the Studebaker bumped over the old Snow Flake railroad spur on Michigan Avenue. "What would have happened if your welding—well, if it didn't go right?"

"Let's not even think about that," Dad said. "I haven't done any welding since 1948. I wasn't even sure I could run a new outfit like that. Thank God that welding apron was cut kind of long, because my knees were shaking so bad I could hardly stand up!"

From Mom, I learned the value of pie and persistence, and that from time to time the healthy thing is to swear and start over. From Dad I learned that a still voice turns away wrath, providing you know what you are talking about. And that was pretty good for just one year.

How Now, Frau Blau?

I don't believe it!" Dad exclaimed.

I followed him around the corner of the old farmhouse to see what was up.

"Look at the privy back there," Dad said. "Mrs. Blau is in it. Sousa doesn't know it, but he's got her trapped. He's going to sell the damn thing right out from under her!"

I was only thirteen, but I could see that the curtain was going up on some sort of farce featuring two classic Wisconsin characters of the middle 1950s—Colonel Sousa and his nemesis Frau Blau—in and around an outhouse near Menchalville in Manitowoc County.

Sousa was the local nickname for an auctioneer who flourished in eastern Wisconsin in those days, selling off the old pioneer farms. He was a short, waddling man, ringed with rolls of fat like the coils of a tuba. But money stuck to him, and he had the other essential tools of a successful country auctioneer: he knew the second-hand price of everything from a Wedgwood teacup to a silo filler, and he had a voice that could carry across two plowed fields and a woodlot. As did many auctioneers in those days, he called himself "Colonel," affected a cane and cowboy boots, and wore a big white Stetson.

I knew a little about Mrs. Blau already, from other auctions I'd gone to with Dad. She was a small-time antique dealer, about seventy and skinny as a rail. She was refreshingly honest and expected everyone she dealt with to be the same, including auctioneers. Dad was stocking our big old house with furniture that had been brought to Wisconsin by the first settlers, and what he couldn't buy at auction, he bought from Mrs. Blau.

As a sideline, he also bid on the old Ithaca, Fox, Lefever, L. C. Smith, and Parker side-by-side shotguns that occasionally turned up in basements and attics. He cleaned them up and resold them, squirreling the profits away for the day when one of the high-grade Lefevers called an "Uncle Dan" would show up on the auction block. As far as Dad was concerned, the Uncle Dan Lefever was the ultimate shotgun, and he wanted one so bad he could taste it.

As we watched, Sousa and a crowd of farmers moved closer to the outhouse. It stood in a clump of overgrown lilacs in the backyard, surrounded by elderly farm machines parked there to be sold. At the moment, Sousa was only twenty feet away from the outhouse, trying to unload a rusty little Farmall Cub tractor.

"Come on, boys," Sousa said, impatiently. "I can't let this machine go for three fifty. They don't make 'em like this anymore!"

"Good thing, too, enso?" said one of the farmers. Sousa ignored this sally. "Three fifty I got, who'll give me four hundred?"

"Three seventy-five," offered the current high bidder, a rangy Norwegian with a cheek full of Copenhagen. Sousa shook his head. "Thank you, Nils, but we're going fifty dollars a throw today, just like the big city. And besides, you're bidding against yourself. Who'll go four hundred?"

Sousa kicked the Farmall's left front tire, spun around, and pointed his cane at a man of about eighty in a snap-brim straw hat. "OK, Romy!" he boomed. "Don't go playing deaf on me now. I know you can hear me and I know you're interested, so let's get off the pot, here. It's four hundred to you."

"But will it start?" Romy asked. "I'll have to drive it home."

"Will it start? Of course it'll start. It started the last time it ran!" shouted Sousa.

A titter of laughter trickled through the crowd of onlookers, but Romy couldn't hear it.

"Well . . . ," Romy said, tentatively.

"Sold!" said Sousa. He slammed his cane down on the tractor's worn leather seat, which split open at the blow and sent shreds of horsehair padding drifting away on the summer breeze.

"Sold for four hundred dollars to Roman Pankratz, item number 176, the Farmall tractor," Sousa said. He tore a sheet of paper off a clipboard and handed it to Romy. "There ya go, Romy," he said. "Signed, sealed, and delivered. Just take that around to the cashier on the porch." Convinced that he had a bargain, Romy beamed contentedly and tottered off to the front of the farmhouse.

Sousa winked at the crowd and clapped his hands to regain their attention. "OK," he said, "right over this way, item number 177, a disk harrow, looks like a John Deere—at least it's green—so who'll start me out . . ."

Sousa stopped in midstride. He was standing in front of the outhouse. "What the hell, boys, they said sell it all, so by God I will!"

He gave the side of the outhouse a resounding whack with his cane. "Here she is, the genuine article, solid red cedar, don't hardly stink at all, she'll come in handy this winter when the septic tank

133

freezes up, just pull out them bolts and you can take her right along, who'll start me out at twenty-five dollars . . ." Sousa smote the privy a second time and looked rapidly back and forth at the crowd for signs of interest.

"Judas priest!" Dad said.

He and I had been looking on, wondering if Mrs. Blau could summon the courage to escape from the outhouse under the eyes of all those men. We never thought Sousa would actually try to sell it, but now that he was, Dad knew it was time to step in.

"Hold on a minute!" Dad said, and elbowed his way through the audience. He bent down and whispered into Sousa's ear.

Sousa turned and gave the outhouse a close look. Then he turned back to Dad and snorted incredulously. "Occupied?" he asked, in a low voice. "Old lady Blau?" Then Sousa's multiple bellies started to shake. He alternated between fits of laughing and coughing. Finally he caught his breath. "I was about to open the door," Sousa said. "God, I wouldn't have missed this for the world!" He saluted Dad with his cane and cleared his throat loudly to reassemble the crowd.

"Forget the outhouse," Sousa said. "Now, then, item 177, the disk harrow. Who'll start me out . . ."

When the harrow was sold, Sousa led the crowd to the barn. Quiet returned to the outhouse and its clump of lilacs. Dad tapped gently on the door with the stem of his pipe. "It's all right, Mrs. Blau, you can come out—they're all gone," he said.

The door eased open about an inch. The metal ferrule of Mrs. Blau's rolled-up umbrella appeared first, followed by her prominent nose. Then she scuttled out, jabbed the umbrella into the soft earth, and smoothed down her long black cotton dress.

"Woo!" Mrs. Blau said, exhaling sharply. "That was close. I was watching through a knothole and I saw what you did. I owe you one, Mr. Crehore."

"Hell, Mrs. Blau, call me Dave," Dad said, grinning. "We haven't got any secrets from each other anymore."

"All right," said Mrs. Blau, "then you may call me Mary."

Dad filled his pipe with Walnut. As he did, Mrs. Blau pulled a crumpled pack of Chesterfields from the pocket of her dress. "Need a light, Mrs.—um, Mary?" Dad asked. Mrs. Blau leaned forward as Dad thumbed his Zippo. She dragged deeply on her cigarette as Dad lit and tamped his pipe. They smiled at each other through the smoke.

"You know, Dave, I just said I owed you one, and I think you can collect on it today," Mrs. Blau said. "One time you asked me to let you know if I ever came across a Lefever shotgun in my travels. Well, there's one here at this farm. It's an Uncle Dan to boot, and it's in pretty good shape. There's a nice Parker, too—and yes, I know what I'm talking about. My father was a gunsmith in Germantown and I used to help him. I grew up with those guns.

"The problem is, the newspaper ad for this auction says three shotguns will be sold, but there's only one actually tagged for sale, and it's an old Crescent Arms wall-hanger. But when I was in the farmhouse looking things over before the auction started this morning, I poked around and found the Parker and the Lefever hidden behind an ironing board in the kitchen closet."

Mrs. Blau glanced over at the barn. "Jolly old Colonel Sousa ain't exactly Santa Claus," she said. "I'll bet you anything he'll pretend to find them after the auction is over and make some kind of a low-ball offer to Gertie, the widow that owns this farm. She needs the money and she'll probably take anything he gives her."

"Dirty work at the crossroads," Dad said. Mrs. Blau looked up at him. "Oh, yes, it happens," she said. "How much money have you got with you?"

"I've got two hundred and fifty in my Lefever fund," Dad said.

"Well, that might be enough," Mrs. Blau said. "I'll make a phone call and see what I can do." She took a final pull on her Chesterfield, ground the butt into the grass with her heel, and strode purposefully to the back door of the farmhouse.

"Good grief," Dad said. "You come out here in the country for a little light entertainment and all of a sudden it's high intrigue! Come on, let's eat our lunch before the egg salad goes bad."

Our Studebaker station wagon was parked along the road in front of the farmhouse. We ate sitting on its tailgate, where we had a good view of the front porch. Something clearly was going on—there were raised voices inside, including Mrs. Blau's raspy tenor, and for a moment we saw her nose-to-nose with Sousa's cashier.

Finally she emerged backward through the screen door, carrying two shotguns. She laid them on a table beside the Crescent Arms gun and some boxes of dishes and kitchenware that were to be sold from the front porch. She saw us and gave us a quick thumbs-up. Dad nodded, opened the glove compartment of the Studie, and removed an envelope full of tens and twenties.

When the auction started up again, Sousa disposed of the dishes for seven dollars, and Romy walked off with the Crescent Arms gun for fifteen. "I gotta lampshade at home that'll just fit this baby," he said, and everyone laughed. Then Sousa looked down and saw the Parker and Lefever. He turned to the cashier and berated him in an angry whisper. The cashier shrugged and nodded toward Mrs. Blau, who stood in the front row of onlookers, fixing Sousa with a narrow-eyed stare.

Sousa recovered his voice. "OK, we're almost done." He walked past the shotguns and picked up one of the cardboard boxes. "Here we got everything you newlyweds need to get started out in life." He rummaged in the box and started pulling things out. "Colander, eggbeater, spatula, lefse roller. Who'll start it out at a quarter?"

"Hey, not so fast!" shouted Mrs. Blau, waving the newspaper ad. "Sell the shotguns!"

Sousa glared at Mrs. Blau and picked up the Lefever. A middle-aged man in a brown fedora hat, who had been looking on from a distance, walked up and joined the crowd.

"All right," Sousa said, "the lady says sell 'em so I will. This here is a Lefever of some kind, looks like a fancy one, so we'll start her out at fifty bucks. Who'll give me fifty?"

"Here!" said the man in the fedora.

"OK, fifty I got, who'll go a hundred?"

"One hundred," Dad said. Sousa scowled; he wasn't expecting any other bidders.

"One fifty!" snapped the fedora.

"Two hundred," Dad said.

The fedora jumped back in. "Two fifty!"

Dad hesitated.

"Three hundred," said Mrs. Blau.

A stunned silence fell over the onlookers. No one in Manitowoc County had ever offered to pay three hundred dollars for a shotgun. In the distance, crows cawed and a windmill squeaked.

"Three hundred is bid!" said Mrs. Blau. Sousa's face turned an ugly crimson. He glanced at the man in the brown fedora.

"Three fifty," said the fedora.

"Four hundred," Mrs. Blau said.

"Four . . . ," said the fedora, but Sousa shook his head almost imperceptibly from side to side. The man in the fedora looked down.

"All done?" said Sousa, scanning the crowd. "Sold! The Lefever shotgun for four hundred dollars to Mrs. Blau. See the cashier when we're through."

Dad turned to me and frowned. "Dammit, there it goes," he said. "That's about as close as I'm ever going to get to an Uncle Dan. Even if Mrs. Blau would sell it, I haven't got four hundred bucks to spend on a shotgun."

Up on the porch, Sousa picked up the Parker. His professional good humor had evaporated. "Now here's another nice one," he said in a gritty voice, "a real Parker, the Old Reliable, nice VHE grade, partridge season comin' up before you know it. Gotta start this one out at a hundred and fifty."

Dad had the fever. "Hundred and fifty," he said.

"Two hundred," countered the fedora.

"Two fifty," Dad said.

The fedora raised his hand. I saw Sousa give that quick shake of the head again. The fedora lowered his hand. There were no other bidders.

"All done?" Sousa shouted. "All done? All right, sold for two hundred and fifty dollars to the man with the pipe!" He waved his hand contemptuously at the colanders and eggbeaters and stalked into the farmhouse, the high heels of his cowboy boots thudding on the worn floorboards. The auction was over.

Mrs. Blau walked briskly over to Dad, carrying the Uncle Dan. "Hurry up, pay for that Parker before Sousa takes a close look at it," she said. "Right away!" Dad went up to the cashier's table, emptied his envelope, and hooked the Parker over his arm.

We headed for the car. Dad raised the Parker to his shoulder and looked down the rib. "Shoot!" he said. "I never should have bid on this thing. It's in beautiful shape, but the stock's got way too much drop—doesn't fit me at all. I'll never be able to hit anything with it, and now I've got to find somebody who'll pay me two hundred and fifty dollars for it!"

"I'll give you that," said Mrs. Blau, who had walked with us. "It doesn't matter if it fits you or not. It's a collector gun. See, I called Gertie over at her daughter's place during lunch—she didn't want to be here and watch her stuff being sold. She said her husband used to hunt with the Lefever, but he won the Parker in a raffle back in 1936 and never shot it, never even took it out of the house. Maybe Sousa knew he was selling a mint-condition gun, maybe he didn't—it doesn't matter, because it's yours now!"

Dad leaned forward and gave Mrs. Blau a resounding kiss on the forehead. "Mary, now I owe you one," he said. "You saved my bacon. More important, you saved my Lefever fund!"

"Oh, that's right, you wanted this Lefever, didn't you," said Mrs. Blau, her face wrinkling into a smile. She took the Parker from Dad and handed him the Uncle Dan.

Dad looked down at her. "What in the hell is going on here?" he asked.

"Well," Mrs. Blau said, "it looks like the man in the brown hat was Sousa's shill. I forced Sousa to auction those guns, so the shill's job was to bid and get them for Sousa. I think he wanted both of those guns for the big-city market, and it looks like he was willing to pay $350 for the Lefever and $200 for the Parker. Now, most of these people here are farmers, and they wouldn't dream of paying 40 bucks for a shotgun, let alone 400. Sousa knew that and he figured he'd get both guns for a song. But he didn't figure on me!" Mrs. Blau laughed a hacking cigarette laugh, like the crumpling of tinfoil. She smiled up at Dad. "If Sousa can have a shill, so can you!"

"More dirty work at the crossroads," Dad said.

"Yes, there are wheels within wheels, even in Menchalville," Mrs. Blau said. "So, let's get down to business. Dave, you've got $250 in the Parker, and I've got $400 in the Lefever. Let's call it an even swap."

"Hell, no, Mary," Dad said. "I owe you $150, and I haven't got it."

"OK," said Mrs. Blau. "Let's just say I'm paying you $150 for services rendered in the backyard. It was worth that much to retain my dignity. Besides, I'll probably make up the difference when I sell the Parker."

Dad shouldered the Uncle Dan and then lowered it and ran his fingers over its intricate engraving and gold inlays. "There's a little wear," he said, "but it fits like a dream." He put the gun in the canvas case he always took to auctions—the "just-in-case case," he called it—and laid it on the backseat of the Studie. Then he turned and took Mrs. Blau's skinny hand in his. "I can't thank you enough, Mary," he said.

"Oh, hell, Dave—the pleasure was all mine. I was almost caught with my . . . well, I was almost caught!"

Dad started up the Studie, but before he drove off he reached back and patted the gun case. Then he laughed and we headed for home.

The Dorking Rooster-Catcher

*B*ack in the 1950s, telegrams and long-distance calls usually meant trouble. We got one of each on a quiet Thursday evening in October 1956, when I was thirteen. They were the opening guns of our first and only day of hunting with an Englishman.

The telegram was delivered just as Mom, Dad, and I were sitting down to supper in the kitchen. A taxi pulled up and the driver honked the horn.

Dad took his pipe from the counter and followed Rip and Nip, our beagles, to the front door. The driver walked up to the porch, carrying a yellow envelope.

"Western Union," he said. "That'll be a dollar." Dad took a single from his wallet and found a fifty-cent piece among the keys and pipe tools in his pocket. Fifty cents was a good tip in 1956.

Back in the kitchen, Dad slit the envelope with his pocketknife. Mom and I waited, barely breathing, expecting the worst. Dad read the narrow strips of paper pasted to the telegraph form. "Well," he said, "don't get excited, everybody's still alive. But we're going to have company for the weekend."

Mom and I looked at the telegram. It was a marvel of economy, from the New York office of the company Dad worked for. It said: PERCIVAL PERKINS LONDON ARR MANITOWOC FRI FOUR THIRTY PM C&NW EXTEND HOSP JONES NY.

Dad translated. "Old man Jones says a guy named Perkins from London is coming on the train tomorrow afternoon. Why, he doesn't say. And we're supposed to extend hospitality. I guess that means we put him up."

The phone rang and I went into the dining room to answer it. "I have a person-to-person call for David Crehore," the operator said. It couldn't possibly have been for me, so I handed the receiver to Dad.

After a couple of minutes Dad hung up. "That was Harry from the Chicago office," he said. "He says this Perkins guy has done us some favors in the past. He had business in Chicago, and now Jones wants us to roll out the red carpet for him. Apparently he likes to hunt birds, so this trip has the earmarks of a junket. I wondered what was going on, and now I know—I'm elected to play grouse guide this weekend."

Mom shifted quickly into hostess mode. "Let's see," she said, "how can we make him feel at home? We have some tea, but beyond that, I'm not sure—English people eat things like herring and kidneys, and I don't think the A&P carries them."

"We can have a beef roast Friday night, a ham on Saturday, grouse on Sunday, and sausages for breakfast. That'll have to do," Dad said. He was really extending hospitality; for us, that was about a month's supply of high-grade meat.

I couldn't wait. Through my reading I had met many fictional Britons, ranging from the Water Rat to Sherlock Holmes, but never a real one. Best of all, it was the weekend of the teachers' convention, there would be no school on Friday, and I wouldn't miss a thing.

By the time I woke up the next morning, Dad had left for the office and Mom was giving the house an unscheduled fall cleaning. She had just started dusting the venetian blinds when Dad came home early. "That's enough, Charlotte," he said. "He won't look at the blinds. The train comes in at four thirty, and I've got to get going. You coming, Davy?"

At the station, Dad drummed his fingers nervously on the steering wheel. Maybe, like me, he was picturing Percival Perkins as a superior being: tall and imperious, impeccably dressed in tweeds, a man who would outshoot us in our own woods, condescend to us ever so politely, and make us feel like the small-town people we were.

Before the tension could grow much more, the train pulled in and we walked to the platform. Six people got off, none of them remotely English. The conductor called, "'Board!" and the engineer gave a double toot on the whistle. Just as the train started moving, a thin middle-aged man jumped down to the platform. He had a tangled mop of grey hair, merry blue eyes, and the long, expressive face of a comedian. He was carrying a dirty gray canvas bag in one hand and a leather leg-of-mutton shotgun case in the other. Dad and I turned toward each other and our eyes met. Could this be the superior being?

"Mr. Perkins?" Dad asked as he strode toward him. "Mr. Crehore?" said the man. They shook hands and Dad introduced me. Perkins wore a wrinkled waxed cotton shooting jacket worn shiny on the elbows and sleeves, a pair of baggy corduroy trousers, and suede desert boots with scuffed toes. "Call me Perce," he said.

I hoisted Perkins's bag to my shoulder and carried it to the car. It was stamped ROYAL MAIL in faded Gothic capitals. Our guest was using an old British mail bag for his luggage, and Dad and I were finally able to relax a little. Regardless of nationality, Perce Perkins was apparently one of us, a member of the perennially underpaid lower middle class.

Dad took his pipe from his shirt pocket. At this cue, Perkins drew a four-ounce tin of Barney's Punchbowle tobacco from the depths of his jacket and held it out to Dad. "Try some of mine, Dave," he said. Dad opened the tin and filled his pipe as Perkins filled his.

Our guest had passed the final test. Punchbowle was a strong Scottish mixture of Virginia and latakia. Dad smoked it when he could afford it and thought highly of anyone else who did. In about five minutes, Percival Perkins had crossed the Atlantic and become a friend. On the way home, we stopped to buy him a hunting license, and I watched as he wrote his name and address on the form: Percival Paul Perkins, 10 Mole St., Dorking, Surrey, England.

When we walked through our front door, we were enveloped in the aroma of roasting beef from a dutch oven on the stove, and between gusts of beef we could smell cinnamon, which suggested an apple pie in the oven. Mom came out of the kitchen, brushing back her hair and drying her hands on her apron.

"Perce, I'd like you to meet my wife, Charlotte . . . ," Dad said, but there was no need for further formality. Perkins took a step toward Mom, reached out and took both her hands in his as though they were about to be married, and looked deeply into her eyes.

"Perce Perkins," he said. "Are you the lass who is responsible for this beautiful home and that delicious food I smell from the kitchen?" Perkins asked.

"Why, I suppose I am," Mom replied, blushing. No one had ever called her a "lass." In thirty seconds, Perkins had won her heart as well.

The adults talked while I did my afternoon chores, feeding the beagles and shooing our bantam chickens into their henhouse in the backyard. Then the four of us sat down to supper. It was good that

Mom had chosen the largest beef roast in the freezer; Perkins ate like a tiger, consuming about a pound of the roast himself and exclaiming over each mouthful.

After supper—and Perkins's second piece of pie—we made plans for the next day.

"We should get up fairly early," Dad said. "The grouse aren't early risers, but we'll need time for breakfast. I can promise you some really fresh eggs—nice little ones from our chickens—and the best pork sausage you ever ate, made right here in town by Herman Dramm. Then we'll head out to Urban Smonjeski's farm about five miles from here. He's got a big woodlot that hasn't been hunted yet this season, so we ought to be able to move a few birds around. That will take us most of the day, if the rain holds off."

"Jolly good," Perkins said. "I'll set my alarm for five o'clock."

Saturday dawned cloudy and gloomy. I was too wound up to need an alarm clock; I put on my hunting clothes and boots and clumped down the stairs. Perkins and Dad were sitting at the kitchen table, drinking coffee, and smoking their morning pipes.

"Dave, it's time to fetch some eggs," Mom said. "About a dozen, if possible." We walked across the backyard to the chicken pen. Dad and I went in, followed by Perkins.

When Dad opened the henhouse, Wilbur and Orville, the roosters, jumped down to the ground, but the eight hens stayed put on their nests. Dad reached under a black-and-white hen in search of an egg. Suddenly, he spun around. "Shoot!" he said. "The roosters are loose."

"Bloody hell," said Perkins. "I must have left the door open. After the buggers!" He ducked through the door frame and began to run after Wilbur and Orville.

"No, no, Perce," Dad shouted, "don't . . ."

Perkins could run surprisingly fast. When he caught up to the roosters they took off with a clatter of wings, heading toward the house.

" . . . chase them."

"Damn!" Perkins said. "I had no idea the little chaps could fly."

"Oh, yes," Dad said. "They fly like eagles."

Wilbur landed near the back door of the house and began scratching in a drift of fallen leaves. But Orville was made of sterner stuff. He kept on flying, locked his wings in a glide, and soared to the peak of the garage roof.

"Oh, Lord," Dad sighed. "Davy, round up Wilbur and put him back. Perce, let's see if we can figure out a way to capture Orville."

Wilbur had been through this before. I chivvied him along quietly, and when he saw the hens he ran stiff-legged to the pen and hopped over the door sill. I latched the pen door and headed for the garage, where the real action was.

When I got there I saw that Dad had devised a strategy involving ladders and landing nets. He stood on a stepladder on one side of the garage, holding a big musky net. Perkins was on the other side, at the top of a wooden extension ladder with a smaller net we used for bass. Orville was having the time of his life, strutting back and forth on the roof peak and shaking his wattles.

"Davy," Dad said, "get a handful of gravel from the driveway, and when I tell you, kind of lob it at Orville. Perce, be ready—there's no telling which way he'll fly. OK, Davy, throw!"

I lobbed the gravel, but Orville had seen through our designs. He took off before the gravel hit the roof and flew directly at Perkins, who fell backward off the ladder, made a desperate sweep with the net, yelled "Oh, blast!" and disappeared below the roofline. There was a second of silence, followed by a thud. "So much for the hospitality," Dad said.

There were about twenty mature oak trees in our yard, and they shed a huge volume of leaves every year. There was nowhere else to put the leaves, so we simply raked them across the grass to the edge of a wooded ravine that ran along one side of the yard. There they lay in great piles, soft and fragrant, accumulating slowly—and it was on one of these piles that Perkins fell.

Dad and I ran around opposite ends of the garage. Perkins was lying on his back; beside him was the net with Orville inside. I got to Perkins first. "Davy," he said, "did you see it? I led the little blighter about two feet and got him on the way down!"

"Never mind that," Dad said. "Are you all right?"

Perkins moved his legs and arms and then sat up. "I believe I'm intact," he said, and began slapping his jacket. "Except—dammit, I've broken my pipe." He took the pieces from a pocket and tried to fit them together. "Oh, poor thing," he said. "It was practically new, and I had such high hopes for it."

"I can fix that, Perce," Dad said. "Davy, go get the box in the glove compartment of the car." The box held a brand-new Hardcastle pipe, fresh from London by way of the little smoke shop in town. Dad gave the pipe to Perkins with a bow. "To the champion rooster-catcher of River Road," Dad said. He picked up Orville, who was still struggling in the net. "If you're sure you're OK, we'd better put this eagle away and get some eggs."

After breakfast Dad, Perkins, Rip, Nip, and I made the fifteen-minute drive to the Smonjeski farm. Rip was getting a little old for chasing rabbits, but his limited range made him an ideal flushing dog, and he had learned to quarter back and forth in front of us like a springer spaniel.

Nip was our retriever. I had taught him to fetch by throwing a tennis ball and giving him a slice of hot dog whenever he brought the ball back. He would only retrieve if I had a hot dog with me and showed it to him first, but the workman is worthy of his hire.

At the farm, we found Urban and his sons finishing up the milking. "I heard partridges drumming in the woods all spring," Urban said, "and back in July I jumped half a dozen of 'em. So you should have something to shoot at. I'll wait 'til you're into the woods before I let the cows out."

Urban's woodlot was surrounded on three sides by a flooded, impenetrable cedar swamp, and we could get to the woodlot only by crossing the pasture and entering from the east. He followed us out to the barnyard and watched as we put our guns together: Dad's 12-gauge Lefever, my Fox 20, and Perkins's handsome old Army and Navy boxlock.

"One thing I should tell you," Urban cautioned. "See that black cow over there, the one with the bell? I just bought her a month ago. She's taken over as boss cow, and she's got a temper, so watch out for her when you come back across the pasture."

Once into the woodlot, we spread out in a skirmish line about twenty yards apart. "Hunt 'em up!" Dad commanded the beagles, and we stepped off into a jungle of hazel brush. We hadn't walked a hundred yards when a grouse flushed almost at Perkins's feet, throwing up a shower of leaves and roaring away through the understory. Perkins shouldered his gun smoothly and touched off a shot.

"That was a grouse, I assume," he said. "I didn't see it fall."

"I heard it hit the ground," Dad said. "Davy, put your retriever on it."

I let Nip sniff a piece of hot dog and commanded him to fetch. He charged off into the woods, and in about a minute he came back with the grouse in his mouth. I held out his chunk of hot dog, and he dropped the dead bird. "Jolly good," Perkins said. "My first ruffed grouse." He smoothed its feathers and tucked it into his coat.

We hunted across the woodlot until we reached the swamp, but didn't move another bird. We walked north a bit and started another swath through the woods. About halfway across, Rip flushed a grouse that flew straight away in front of me, an easy shot. I dropped it, and Nip made another retrieve, holding the bird until I gave him some more hot dog.

We hunted back and forth across the woodlot for two more hours without flushing another grouse. "I think they can smell the rain coming," Dad said. "They're heading for the swamp to roost."

We trudged on a bit farther, and then the last bird of the day flushed in front of Dad. It ducked behind a big hemlock and banked hard left toward the swamp. Dad waited it out and killed it at thirty-five yards with the Lefever's left barrel. As Nip delivered the grouse, rain began pattering on the leaves overhead. "We'd better hunt our way back to the pasture and decide what to do when we get there," Dad said.

When we got to the pasture we found that Urban's cows had heard us coming. About fifty Holsteins were gathered just across the fence, giving us the once-over. We unloaded our guns and I leashed the beagles while Dad and Perkins lit their pipes, smoking them upside down to keep the rain from putting them out. More rain clouds were scudding toward us from the east.

"Well," Dad said, "I'm as wet as I care to be. I'm ready to call it a day if you are."

"No argument," Perkins said. "But I wonder about that black cow. She's right over there," he said, "and she's watching us."

Perkins handed Dad his gun. "I'll cross the fence and see what she does," he said. I spread the strands of barbed wire so Perkins could squeeze between them. He walked a few yards into the pasture, but the black cow didn't like him. She shook her head menacingly and started for him at a brisk walk, her vast udder swinging from side to side. Perkins waved his arms at her. "G'wan, you old git! Shoo! Be gone!" he yelled, but the black cow kept on coming. Perkins started walking backward and looked at us over his shoulder. "Spread the wire again, I'm coming through," he said. At the last possible moment he turned his back on the advancing cow and crawled between the strands.

Perkins relighted his pipe. The black cow had her head across the top wire of the fence and was pawing the ground like El Toro. "It's a standoff," he said. "We can't walk through the swamp, and we can't cross the pasture as long as that old bitch is here."

Then he smiled. "Half a minute, I've got an idea." He walked slowly toward the black cow, speaking in a crooning, singsong voice: "Easy, girl, I'll soon sort you, you're in for a big surprise." When he was within a foot of her he took a deep, whistling draw at his pipe and blew a dense cloud of Punchbowle smoke into her nostrils.

"Baw!" bleated the black cow. She reared up, snorting, and cantered off to the far corner of the pasture, her bell clanging and the rest of the cows thundering after her.

Dad and I were dumbstruck. "Where did you learn to handle cows?" Dad asked.

"Oh, I don't know a thing about cows, but I know a lot about tobacco," Perkins said. "I believe it was the latakia she didn't like. My wife doesn't care for it either."

The two men knocked the ashes out of their pipes, looked at each other, and grinned. "Well, I hope you had a good time today, Perce," Dad said. "Too bad you only got one shot, but in Wisconsin a bird a day is a good average, any way you slice it. Three shots, three birds— we're perfect."

Driving home, Dad made an admission. "Perce," he said, "I've got to say I'm relieved. Before I met you I assumed you'd be some kind of upper-class hotshot who would make Davy and me look like bumpkins."

Perkins laughed. "Dave, I was thinking the same sort of thing, but the other way round," he said. "I had you figured for a back-woodsman who would make a fool of a city boy like me. But I guess bird hunters are all cut from the same bolt."

It rained all night and was still raining Sunday morning, so we ate a lazy breakfast of bantam eggs and leftover ham.

Mom broiled the grouse for lunch and then we drove Perkins to the railroad station. We never saw him again, but he and Dad exchanged Christmas cards and tins of tobacco until Dad died in 1984. Sometimes the cards had pictures of grouse, sometimes cows or chickens.

The Man of Action

Jeez, you should see the shiner my old man's got! He was in a fight in the tavern last night, and he really caught one. But he knocked the other guy down so I guess he won."

The school bus that hauled us country kids rattled down Waldo Boulevard on its way to Woodrow Wilson Junior High in Manitowoc. In the seat beside me, Frank was laying it on thick, making his old man's scuffle at Art and Helen's Tap sound like a title fight.

But in a way I was jealous of Frank. He had an old man that hung around taverns, got into fights, and bragged about them afterward, a tough guy who didn't take crap from anybody. My dad, on the other hand, took a lot of crap as cochairman of the Saint Paul's Methodist building committee.

Not that Dad was a milquetoast. In college, he had played the line on both sides of the ball in the days of leather helmets. And he spent the late '30s as an engineer on a Great Lakes ore boat.

No, Dad was no softy, but he wasn't exactly a man of action, either. There was an Irish temper behind his smile and ever-present pipe, but few people saw it. Words, patience, and humor were his tools, and if they didn't work the first time, he'd try them again. "Patience is a virtue, find it if you can, seldom in a woman, never in a man," he used to say.

I put all that out of my mind as the bus pulled up at Wilson. I had bigger worries that September, starting with a C in geometry that would probably get worse before it got better. And in any case, my jerry-built idea of manhood was about to be knocked flat at Horicon Marsh, the big refuge in east central Wisconsin that was becoming famous for its goose hunting.

In the spring and fall, immense flocks of Canada geese gathered at Horicon, and Dad loved Canadas the way most people love sunsets. Back in the midfifties, Canadas weren't as common as they are now, and even when we were in the thick of a grouse cover, he would stop and look up when chanting flocks passed overhead. He'd stand there, listening, until they were out of sight.

That fall, Dad decided to try some goose hunting at Horicon. In those days the Horicon season didn't open until November, but Dad was a thorough sort of man and got an early start.

In August, he bought three books about goose hunting and read them front to back at the kitchen table, smoking his pipe and taking notes. On September evenings, while I duked it out with Pythagoras, Dad was down in the basement, jigsawing sheets of Masonite into the outlines of geese. Later, turpentine vapor filled the house as he turned each outline into a simplified oil painting of a Canada with a movable head and neck. When he had made thirty of these profile decoys, Dad brought home a couple of navy surplus sea bags to carry them in, and got out the goose calls.

He had bought the calls by mail order from Herter's, with an instruction book and a 78-rpm record of expert calling. During

October, we spent a half hour most nights playing the record on the Magnavox and calling along with it. Our rehearsals were loud and repetitive; they sent our beagles into ecstasy and Mom into the kitchen.

Then Dad brought home two goose guns in plain brown wrappers, a well-used but sturdy Winchester Model 21 side-by-side for him and a Model 12 pump for me. In late October, we practiced on the skeet field, stepping back thirty yards from the targets. Over and over, I tried the long crossing shots from stations three, four, and five. "Lead 'em the length of your gun," Dad told me.

Most goose hunting stories start when the hunters struggle out of bed in the cold, dark hours of early morning, but if you hunted at Horicon in those days you had to get going the night before. The federal government had built goose blinds around the edges of the northern part of the refuge, and they were assigned to hunters on a first-come, first-served basis before dawn each morning. To secure a good blind, you had to get your car into line on a country road near the marsh by one or two in the morning, and that meant leaving Manitowoc no later than nine thirty.

And so, on a Friday night in late November, we hit the road to Horicon in our Studebaker station wagon crammed with decoys, guns, ammunition, and bags of lunch.

Nothing much was going on in Valders and Chilton as we passed through. Along the east shore of Lake Winnebago, the little towns of Brothertown, Calumetville, and Pipe had gone to bed, and by the time we got to Fond du Lac, the Blatz and Old Style signs were winking out as the bars closed. Then I fell asleep until Dad pulled into the waiting line of cars at the refuge.

He hopped out and counted the cars ahead of us.

"Eight, nine, ten—we're eleventh in line, I guess that's pretty good for a Saturday morning," Dad said. "Get some more sleep if you can."

But I couldn't. Up and down the line, drivers were idling their engines to warm up their cars. Men and dogs, their breath smoking in the cold, ran errands into the cornfields along the road. One guy had set up an army cot on the shoulder. He was sound asleep with a big Chesapeake Bay retriever curled up under the cot.

At 4:00 a.m., the line began to move. We drew up to a sort of roadside stand where the blinds were assigned.

"We want blind 56 if it isn't taken," Dad said. A friend of his had gotten a goose from blind 56 on Thursday morning.

"Fifty-six it is," the warden said. He checked our licenses and duck stamps, wrote down our names, and gave us a hand-drawn map. And off we went, the Studie bottoming out on the rutted clay.

After a mile or two of back roads, our headlights jabbed into a small, muddy parking lot that served blinds 55, 56, and 57. Following the map, Dad and I lugged our goose gear down a steep hill into the darkness.

Blind 56 was an open-topped, six-by-six-foot structure of snow fence and cornstalks about a quarter mile from the parking lot. Dad walked around with a flashlight to get the lay of the land.

"Let's set up the decoys in that picked cornfield just up the hill," he said, shouldering the first bag. He laid the folded decoys on the ground, spaced a few feet apart in a curving, upwind V, and heeled their wooden stakes into the soil. My job was to follow along behind him and attach the decoys to the stakes with carriage bolts and wing nuts.

Setting up profile decoys is hard work, and it turns into desperate work when dawn sneaks in from the east and threatens to expose you. I had the feeling that thousands of beady black Canada goose eyes were watching me as I spun the last few wing nuts and ducked into the blind.

"OK," Dad said, "I've paced it off, and that big willow over there is about forty yards away. So is the fence and the far edge of the decoy spread. We'll cripple birds any farther away than that, so don't shoot at anything that is beyond the decoys, the tree, or the fence."

"The best part is that we've got the place to ourselves," Dad said. Sure enough, blind 55, about two hundred yards north of us, was empty, and so was 57, the same distance to the south.

We took our guns from their cases and loaded them, poured coffee into the steel caps of our thermos bottles, and unwrapped a couple of Mom's bologna and mayonnaise sandwiches. "Might as well have some breakfast now," Dad said, "because they're going to start moving any minute."

And as though they had been waiting for his cue, ten thousand Canadas lifted themselves from the marsh with a wild fanfare and began to wheel chaotically on the western horizon. As we watched, the whirling galaxy of geese broke into flocks and subflocks spinning off to all points of the compass.

"Here comes a string of about twenty right at us," Dad whispered. "They're climbing to get over the hill, so we've gotta call them down into our decoys. I won't shoot this first time. Let's start calling and I'll tell you when to stand up. Remember, nothing over forty yards!"

Hunkered down in the blind and watching the geese through holes in the cornstalks, we began the "hink, honk, hink-honk, honk, hink-honk" duet that Herter's had assured us would sound like dozens of geese.

Apparently it did. The birds were headed straight for our decoy spread, slowing, gliding, dropping lower. Then they were so close that I couldn't see them through the stalks and slats of the blind. "Stop calling!" Dad said, and in the sudden silence I could hear the hiss of wind in the pinions of the geese overhead.

"Now!" Dad said.

I stood up and spun around toward the decoys. Dad's Masonite flock and our five-dollar calls had fooled all of the geese in the string.

They were dropping in for a landing, talking to each other, their great webbed feet extended.

Then they saw me. Twenty geese accelerated wildly in all directions. I picked a goose headed to my right and swung the Winchester through him. On the skeet field, it would have been a station three high-house shot, and I could usually hit those. I led the goose a gun-length and yanked the shotgun's trigger.

The gun barked and bucked and I pumped the action so hard that the ejected shell flew completely out of the blind. But I didn't need a second shot. The goose folded, fell end-over-end to the ground, and bounced, stone dead.

I stood open-mouthed. My ears roared. The goose lay there, crumpled among the decoys. Dad was saying something. I couldn't hear him.

"What?" I shouted.

"Put your safety back on," Dad said. "And go pick up your bird."

All was well in blind 56. Dad congratulated me on my shooting. I congratulated him on the high quality of his decoys. We admired my goose and polished off some more coffee and bologna sandwiches.

And then trouble arrived, in the form of two guys who walked down the hill to blind 55. They wore ordinary work clothes and carried uncased shotguns, several boxes of shells, and what looked like a bottle in a paper bag. No calls. No decoys.

Dad hadn't killed his goose yet, and small groups of Canadas were still trading back and forth on the borders of the marsh. But whenever some geese headed our way the men in 55 would scare them off by firing shot after shot at impossible distances.

An hour passed. Three times we called geese almost close enough, and three times we were thwarted by the sky busters in blind 55. Their supply of ammunition seemed unlimited. Finally, after firing at about a dozen geese apiece, they scratched down two.

The Horicon goose limit in those days was one goose per hunter per season; that meant the men in 55 were through for the year, but they showed no signs of leaving. "Well," Dad said, "I'm sick of running a guide service for those buggers. Let's give it another hour and then pack up."

I was half asleep when Dad poked me. "Here comes a little string from the south," he said, "real low. Don't call. I'll try to get one before those guys see them."

When the geese were as close as they were going to get, Dad stood up and shot a big one going away at forty yards. It died in the air, falling about halfway between blind 55 and us.

"At last," Dad said. "Now, do your old father a favor and go get that goose."

I squeezed out of the blind and walked toward Dad's bird. Then I saw one of the men from blind 55 heading for it too, at a dead run. I sped up, got to the goose first, and picked it up by the legs.

The man from blind 55 came puffing up and took the goose by the neck. "Give me that goose, kid," he yelled. "I shot it!"

I froze, my heart hammering. I didn't let go of my end of the goose. "The hell you did," I said. "My dad shot it."

"Gimme the goose, you little puke, or I'll knock you on your ass," said the man from blind 55.

"Why don't you pick on somebody your own size," said Dad from behind me. I hadn't heard him come up. There was an unfamiliar edge to his voice. "Davy, step aside," Dad said.

I dropped the goose's legs and scuttled sideways, glad to be out from between five hundred pounds of angry men. I took a good look at the guy from blind 55.

He was a man of action all right, the first I had ever seen up close. He was a little bigger than Dad and twenty years younger, with a stubble of beard and a smell of brandy on him that would cut varnish. He dropped the goose, cursed, and swung a wild right hook at Dad's head. Dad's left hand shot out and stopped the punch in midair. His right fist, which measured six inches from side to side, was poised a foot from the man's face.

It was the moment I had been waiting for. This was the kind of violence you seldom saw in Methodists. Boy, would I have a story to tell on the school bus!

But Dad never threw his punch. Instead, he maintained his grip on the man's right fist and pushed him away. The man stumbled and fell heavily into a half-frozen puddle.

"Take the damn goose and get back in your blind," Dad said. The man obeyed. We turned and walked away.

What was this? It was Dad's goose! Why did he let the man take it? Had we won or lost? My emotions wound themselves into a pretzel. Back at our blind, Dad grabbed the decoy bags. "You pull 'em up and I'll bag 'em," he said. I didn't argue. Within forty-five minutes we were in the parking lot with all our gear. When it was stowed away, we sat on the Studie's tailgate to finish our lukewarm coffee.

As soon as Dad's pipe was drawing well, I figured it was OK to ask a question.

"Jeez, Dad, why didn't you hit that guy?" I asked.

"Because he was drunk, and he was afraid," Dad said. "And this is supposed to be hunting, not kids in a sandbox."

"Why did you let him have the goose?"

"Because it put him over the limit, that's why," Dad said.

Some geese were moving again, and as we watched from the hilltop, the men in 55 fired salvoes at a passing flock.

"You hear that?" Dad said. "One of those guys fired five shots in a row, and the other one at least four. They've been doing that all morning, and it's against the law." Obviously the men in 55 hadn't bothered to plug the magazines of their guns. That made two more violations. They were getting away with murder; it wasn't fair, and I said as much.

159

"Don't worry about it," Dad said. "I've still got my goose tag. If you can stand another day of this, we'll come back next Saturday and you can help me call one in. Now let's go find a game warden."

Dad fired up the Studie and we headed out of the parking lot. I was dead tired and wildly excited at the same time. What a day! I had killed my first goose. And Dad had ended a fight with nothing more than a stare and a shove. I no longer had a juicy story for the school bus, but somewhere in the back of my fourteen-year-old brain, a new idea of manhood was peeking over the horizon.

We hadn't gone more than a hundred yards when we saw a brown Chevrolet pickup bouncing down the road in our direction. Dad waved and the truck stopped alongside us. We recognized the federal warden who had assigned us our blind that morning.

"I think you should check blind 55," Dad said. "There are two men in there with three geese, they're still shooting, and I don't believe either gun is plugged."

"We'll see about that," the warden said. He looked at my goose, made sure it was tagged, and then drove on to the parking lot we had just left. Soon we saw him walking down the path to blind 55. Dad got out his binoculars and we passed them back and forth to watch the little drama unfolding on the hillside below us.

The warden unloaded both men's guns and pulled the magazine caps. There were no plugs. He looked at one goose in the blind and found two others that had been hidden in a clump of cattails. Then he started writing citations. He wrote a lot of citations.

Dad lit his pipe and shook out the match. "And what did you learn from this wonderful morning?" he asked.

"Patience is a virtue?" I replied.

"No. The lesson for today is that revenge is sweet, especially when somebody else does it for you. And it looks like Uncle Sam has just delivered a swift kick to the wallet."

No Fair!

On a wet Sunday afternoon in early June 1957, I was sitting at the dining room table in our old house on River Road, drinking a glass of milk, and paging through the *Milwaukee Journal* comics section.

It was raining too hard to go fishing, I was fourteen years old and bored, and the comics weren't helping much. As usual, Dick Tracy was fighting crime and talking on his 2-Way Wrist Radio, the Dragon Lady was plotting Oriental intrigue, Fearless Fosdick was shooting neat round holes in the bad guys, and evil commies were kidnapping Little Orphan Annie while her dog Sandy looked on helplessly, saying "Arf."

I flipped to *Pogo* and *Li'l Abner,* the only strips I actually liked. *Pogo* was always good for a laugh, and I routinely checked out *Li'l Abner* to gawk at Daisy Mae, Moonbeam McSwine, Stupefyin' Jones, and the other Dogpatch girls in their incredibly tight and skimpy clothes.

I was looking them over when Dad came in from the kitchen and handed me three envelopes of Burpee seeds—watermelons, acorn squash, and cucumbers—and a slender book on raising vegetables.

"Project for you this summer," Dad said. "Spade up a patch behind the shed and plant 'em according to the instructions in the book." Cripes, I thought, school just got out Tuesday and already he has me digging.

"It'll be a money-making proposition," Dad said. "I'll pay you fifty cents for every watermelon that's big enough to eat, a quarter apiece for the squash, and a nickel each for the cucumbers. And if you enter some of them in the county fair, you'll get an exhibitor's pass that will let you in free every day, whether you win a ribbon or not. That's two bucks saved right there, and if you're lucky with your crops you'll have all the money you need for the fair."

That got my attention; I was a fair fanatic. The Manitowoc County Fair was held six days each August about a mile and a half from our place, and I never missed a day. It ranked right up there with Christmas and Thanksgiving as one of the high points of my year. In Manitowoc, the fair was as close as we ever got to the bright lights.

To my surprise the vegetables flourished. By the middle of August I had a dozen big watermelons, two rows of plump and profitable squash, and about a hundred cucumbers that met the strict standards set by my book: four inches long, an inch in diameter, and warty. Bigger cucumbers, the book said, were full of seeds and too large to be conveniently pickled and put into Mason jars.

I decided to enter my cucumbers, and it was with great expectations that I paid the one-dollar entry fee, signed a form, and picked up the pass. On Monday, the first day of the fair, I put a paper plate with five carefully chosen cukes on a long table in the Armory with dozens of others, mostly huge and undesirable. Apparently the people who grew them hadn't read the book.

The largest cucumbers of them all, great swollen things like green submarines, were next to mine. They had been entered by someone named Laura Larsen. I pictured her as a chubby, snub-nosed little girl in a starched pinafore who would pout when I walked off with the blue ribbon.

I left the Armory and took a walk around the fairgrounds while the morning was still fresh and cool. On the north side of the midway, seriously sunburned men were walking slowly back and forth, assembling the Ferris wheel, the Tilt-A-Whirl, the Scrambler, the Octopus, and other large and rickety rides.

Across the midway from the rides was a row of pitch-and-toss stands. They were already open for business, but I passed them by. I had been cruelly cheated by them in previous years, and I knew from bitter experience that I couldn't lob a five-inch wooden hoop over a four-inch post from a distance of ten feet.

I had also learned that I couldn't throw a baseball hard enough to knock over three white bottles stacked in a pyramid. I suspected that the bottles were made of lead, and I was pretty sure the baseballs had been doctored as well. The only really good curve I ever threw was with one of those baseballs.

Just ahead, however, was my intended victim, the wizened old crook who ran the shooting gallery. In 1956 I had spent six dollars there without winning a thing and went away baffled. With my own Savage bolt-action single shot .22 I could hit bottle caps at fifty yards, so my marksmanship wasn't the problem. For months I wondered how I could shoot so well at home and so poorly at the fair. Finally I asked Dad about it.

"Those gallery guns are so worn out they shoot around corners," he said, "and I'll bet the rear sights are buggered up besides. Annie Oakley couldn't hit a bull in the ass with one of them. If I were you I wouldn't bother. Otherwise, you'll have to find some way to sight in the rifle without being noticed."

I plotted revenge while I was weeding my cucumbers that summer, and now, on the opening morning of the fair, it was time to settle the score. My heart thudded as I walked up to the counter and paid half a buck for ten shots with an old Winchester pump-action .22. I lifted the rifle to my shoulder, picked a freshly painted metal target about thirty feet away, and held the sights in the middle of it.

I pulled the trigger and the slow-moving little bullet hit the target with a clank a fraction of a second later. With the sharp eyes of youth I saw a small gray mark appear at the point of impact, about an inch below the center and two inches to the right. I waited until the crook was talking to another customer, turned away, and bent the rear sight up and to the left with the screwdriver blade of my Boy Scout knife. I fired another trial shot and found that I was dead on for windage and about a quarter-inch low, which was close enough for my purposes.

Now that I was sighted in I began some serious shooting, pausing now and then to let the barrel cool. I shot up four dollars worth of .22s and won two pink teddy bears, three packs of Pall Mall cigarettes, a Benrus wristwatch, and an angry look from the crook when he handed over the prizes.

Vengeance was mine! As a member of the Methodist Youth Fellowship, I knew that vengeance was supposed to be the Lord's, but I didn't give a damn. I was walking about a foot above the sawdust when I headed down the midway with my loot.

After a while, though, I got tired of carrying the teddy bears, so I gave them to a woman who was pushing a couple of little kids in a stroller. I sold the Pall Malls for fifty cents to a teenage thug with a greasy ducktail haircut and a black leather jacket, turning a small profit.

Then I wound up my Benrus, and when the noon whistle at the shipyard blew I set both hands straight up. I waited impatiently for the minute hand to move, but it didn't. Five minutes later it was still noon. The watch probably needed a little bump to get it started, I figured, so I took it off my wrist and tapped it against the heel of my shoe. The back of the watch came off and a cascade of gears and springs fell into the sawdust.

At that moment somebody grabbed me from behind and spun me around. It was the thug in the black leather jacket. "Where the hell didya get them cigarettes?" he shouted. "Chrissake, they must be ten years old! The tobacco just falls right out! Gimme my money back!"

"OK, OK," I said. I dug out two quarters and handed them over. "What are ya, some kinda crook?" accused the thug. He waved his fist in my face. "I oughta pound ya," he added.

I walked away as fast as dignity would allow. So much for my revenge. I had shot up eight of my watermelons with nothing to show for it, and if the Methodist Youth Fellowship ever found out they would laugh themselves silly. There was a lesson in all this, but I put it out of my mind and kept walking.

The livestock barns were next: sheep, swine, and cattle. It was always best to visit the livestock barns early in the fair, because they got pretty ripe after three or four days of hot weather. The sheep barn was full of big blatting rams and ewes, but in a back corner was a small pen containing a single lamb, a late-born, knock-kneed little charmer with a black face and socks. I looked at the card stapled to the wooden gate. "Breed: Hampshire lamb," it read. "Entrant: Laura Larsen, St. Nazianz, Wisc."

It was the little girl with the big cucumbers! The lamb wobbled over to me, and as I reached down to scratch its head I heard a sweet feminine voice. "Isn't he cute?" it said.

I turned around, expecting the chubby third-grader I had imagined. Instead I was face to face with a Nordic princess. Her long blonde hair was braided into a pigtail that reached to her tiny waist and she wore jeans almost as tight as Daisy Mae's, rolled up to reveal trim ankles. The front of her red and white checked blouse had bumps that were a preview of coming attractions. I was smitten. No, I was overwhelmed.

Laura slipped through the gate and sat down cross-legged on the straw. She called the lamb to her and it jumped into her lap. She rubbed noses with it and then smiled up at me. I stood there with my mouth open, possibly drooling. I had just discovered that nothing is more appealing to a fourteen-year-old boy than a fourteen-year-old Norwegian farm girl with a lamb in her lap.

"Do you have sheep in the fair?" she asked.

"No, no sheep," I stammered. "Cucumbers, but no sheep."

She rubbed noses with the lamb again and cooed at it. "His name is Barney. I just think lambs are so cute," she said.

"Yeah, real cute," I said. Especially when sitting in that lap.

Some other farm girls walked up and began talking to Laura. Compared to her, they were ugly as trolls. Dammit, I thought, the moment is slipping away and I'm standing here turning colors like a barber pole. The trolls showed no sign of leaving, so I staged a strategic retreat. "I'll be seeing you," I said, grinning like an idiot.

"It was very nice meeting you," she said. "My name is Laura."

"Yeah, I know," I said. "My cucumbers are right next to yours."

"Oh, are they?" she said. "Well, good-bye. Barney and I will be here until Sunday." It was an invitation to return, and she flashed me another one of those smiles.

"Yeah, good-bye," I said, and got out of there.

I stumbled through the swine barn in a romantic stupor. Usually pigs interested me; they had big bodies, short legs, and small, worried eyes like some people I knew. But I barely noticed them. "Laura Larsen, Laura Larsen," I muttered. There was poetry in that name.

When I emerged from the stifling heat of the swine barn I was beaded with sweat and filled with resolve. I shall return, I vowed, quoting General MacArthur. I shall return with a little savoir faire. I shall return and tell her my name.

After supper I rode my bike back to the fairgrounds. My first stop was the sheep barn. Barney was alone in his pen, and as I turned to leave, a grandmotherly woman sitting in front of an adjoining pen of Merinos spoke to me.

"Looking for Laura?" she asked.

"Sort of," I said.

"Sort of, my foot," she said, with a knowing smile. "She and her mother are out walking around the fairgrounds. You might run into her, enso?"

"Yeah, maybe," I said, but I didn't think much of my odds. It was the first night of the fair and at least two thousand assorted shipyard workers, high-school kids, farmers, and good-natured drunks were clogging the midway. I decided to lurk there, walking back and forth and hoping that Laura would pass by on her way to tuck Barney in for the night.

I bought a bag of salt-water taffy and started looking for a blonde pigtail. But Laura and her mother were nowhere to be seen, and after about an hour I gave up and got in line for a ride on the Scrambler.

I liked the Scrambler because it didn't hurl its victims into the air or spin them around like the other rides. Instead it did its evil work at ground level. The passengers sat in aluminum cars with slippery bench seats and were thrown violently from side to side while rotating around a central column, constantly accelerating and decelerating.

The idea was to ride the Scrambler with a girl, maneuvering her so that she sat on the end of the seat. The operator would yank a lever, feeding power to the Scrambler's huge motor. You would fly off to the left, stop suddenly, pause for a second, and then rocket back to the right. When the car slowed down, momentum slammed you into the girl, when it sped up she slammed into you, and a good time was had by all.

The Scrambler had just come to a stop when I heard that sweet voice again. Laura and her mother, a grim six-footer, had joined the line behind me. I got another high-voltage smile from Laura, making three for the day.

"Hi, Dave, are you having a good time?" she asked. "I got your name from your cucumbers—we were just looking at them."

Hot blood shot to my face. She cared! She had walked the entire length of the fairgrounds to find out who I was!

Laura introduced me to her mother, who gave me a quick once-over. "Dave's cucumbers were cute," Laura said. "Weren't they, Mom?"

"I suppose," her mother said. I guessed she didn't think much of boys who entered cucumbers in the fair. Cows, maybe, but not cucumbers.

The Scrambler was filling up fast. I pulled out a handful of my squash money and bought three tickets. When we boarded our car I tried to sit next to Laura, but her mother wedged herself between us.

What happened next was the longest and fastest Scrambler ride I had ever experienced. When we got up to speed, the operator jammed the throttle wide open and walked off. The ride went on and on. We were really getting our money's worth, but instead of colliding pleasantly with Laura, I was battering her mother's large and bony hips.

I held on with all my strength, but I couldn't resist the massive G-forces of the Scrambler, which had shifted itself into overdrive and was throwing us back and forth at maniacal speed. Laura shrieked delightedly while her mother fixed me with a look of silent disgust. Apparently she thought I was crashing into her on purpose.

Finally the operator came back, carrying a large paper cup of Kingsbury beer. He looked at his watch and grabbed the lever. When we got off the Scrambler Laura's mother walked away without a word, her long legs pumping.

"Wait up, Mom," Laura said. "I'm dizzy." When we caught up with her, I handed out taffy as a peace offering. Laura's mother declined at first but finally gave in, took a piece, and began to chew. Then she gagged and turned away from us. She stuck two fingers into her mouth and pulled out a dripping gob of taffy. A large and expensive-looking chunk of broken bridgework was imbedded in it. She put the gob into her purse.

"Come, Laura, we muth be going," she said, whistling through the gap in her front teeth like a hockey player. All I could do was stand there as she strode rapidly down the midway, pulling Laura behind her.

Something my great-grandfather Albert once told me popped into my head: "Never get serious about a girl until you've had a look at her mother," he said. "A real close look. Girls turn into their mothers after a while." Laura Larsen had lost a little of her luster.

The next morning I hung around the sheep barn, but Laura was always guarded, sometimes by her mother, sometimes by the trolls. When I walked by, her mother glared and the trolls tittered. And there were no more smiles from Laura. She acted like I was invisible, and I soon found out why: a new admirer had appeared, a tall, good-looking kid of fifteen or sixteen. Compared to him, I was grubby and strictly ordinary. From then on he practically lived in the sheep barn and Laura stuck to him like flypaper.

The fair went on, day after day, but a lot of the fun had gone out of it. Just before closing time on Thursday night I made one last trip to Barney's pen. He was sleeping, and no one was around except the woman I had talked to on opening day.

She gave me a sympathetic look. "In case you're wondering," she said, "that tall kid lives down the road from Laura. His father owns four hundred acres and milks about seventy-five head, and he's a seed corn dealer besides—the local kingpin. Laura's mother practically has her married off to the kid already. But you still have a chance, enso?"

"Yeah," I said, without much conviction. I couldn't compete with the young prince of St. Nazianz and I knew it.

Friday was vegetable-judging day. I waited in the doorway of the Armory as the cucumber judge moved slowly up and down, distributing ribbons. When he was done I walked calmly to the long table of cukes, fully expecting a blue ribbon, although a red ribbon for second place would be OK, too.

But when I got to them, I saw that a terrible mistake had been made. The First Premium Blue Ribbon was draped across Laura's submarines. My splendid entries did not even get honorable mention.

The cucumber judge was on the other side of the table. He was a thin man of about fifty who wore horn-rimmed glasses and parted his hair in the middle. I worked up a little nerve.

"I got a book that says cucumbers are supposed to be like these," I said, pointing to my plate. "But you gave the blue ribbon to some that are way too big."

The judge looked back and forth at my cucumbers and Laura's. Then he shuffled through a pad of entry forms on a clipboard. "I think I see the problem," he said. "You entered your cucumbers in the wrong division."

He handed me my entry form and put his finger on some small type I hadn't read when I signed it. "This form is for the table division, and in that division, the bigger the better," he said. "Yours are pickling cucumbers. If you had entered them in the pickling division, you would have taken first prize. Those are beautiful little cukes for pickles."

170

"But . . . ," I said.

"No buts," said the judge. "Rules are rules."

He walked on. I was alone at the cucumber table, and I said some things about rules and the judge and the shooting gallery and Laura and her mother and the prince that would have gotten me drummed out of the Methodist Youth Fellowship. I felt a lot better when I was through.

Outside, a cool breeze was blowing off Lake Michigan, and towering white clouds were drifting by under a sky of perfect blue. As I headed back to the midway I added four axioms to my meager collection of wisdom:

> Rules are rules.
> Always read the fine print.
> Never try to cheat a cheater.
> Always take a close look at the mother.

Along the way I met Lois, a girl I knew from Woodrow Wilson Junior High. She was wearing Bermuda shorts and a sweatshirt, and her light brown hair was cut short for the summer. She was no princess, but I was no prince. I told her about my cucumber fiasco and she didn't laugh, which endeared her to me.

"I didn't enter anything in the fair this year," she said, "but my mom won two blue ribbons for her pies, one for apple and one for lemon meringue."

Things were looking up already.

Hand in hand, we walked to the Scrambler. The only seats left were between two jolly plump ladies who smelled of beer. I gave the operator the last of my watermelon money and Lois and I whirled away, alternately squashing and being squashed by the ladies, who were having the time of their lives. And so were we. Two days of the fair were left, and they were bound to be worth the price of admission.

The Wanderer

Tuck was the dog that came in out of the rain.

He moved firmly into our lives on a wet Monday night in April 1959. Five months later, on an evening in early autumn, he moved on.

I was sixteen in 1959. The night he showed up, I had been to a high school meeting that gave me an excuse to take the Studebaker and hang around Late's Bar-B-Q for a while afterward. It was about eleven o'clock and raining hard when I drove into the open door of our garage.

I hadn't seen anything when I pulled in, but as soon as I got out of the car a dog started whimpering and jumping up.

For a minute I thought it was one of our two elderly beagles, Rip and Nip. Maybe Dad had forgotten to let them in. But that couldn't be; neither of them had enough sense to hide in the garage when it

172

rained. No, I knew from experience that when the beagles were left outside in bad weather they would huddle on the flagstones of our back porch, shivering and waiting to be remembered.

I reached down and felt a short wiry coat stretched tightly over ribs I could count with a fingertip. I knelt and the dog leapt into my arms, licking my face with such passion that I had to close my eyes. Holding him, I discovered a little more: male, no collar, maybe twenty-five pounds, with generous ears that stuck up from his head like a terrier's and then flopped down like a hound's.

I cradled him in my arms and carried him through the rain to the back door. My plan was to sneak him into the kitchen before Rip and Nip caught on, but they were way ahead of me. As soon as I eased the door open and came inside, there was a clatter of claws as the beagles skidded through the kitchen and surged down the back hall.

They were flabbergasted to find someone new in their house. They walked around stiff-legged and their back hair rose in ridges, but there was no dogfight. Instead, the newcomer initiated a sniffing ceremony. He allowed himself to be investigated and then examined the beagles. Tails wagged all around, and it appeared that they were going to get along.

I shut the beagles in the dining room so I could be alone in the kitchen with the little dog. I sat down on the linoleum floor and he climbed into my lap. He was brown and black, with a coat as dense and curly as steel wool. I guessed he was a cross between a hound of some kind and a wire-haired fox terrier, and probably not more than a year old. After a couple of minutes he hopped off my lap and sat in front of our Coldspot refrigerator, looking expectantly over his shoulder at me, then at the fridge, then at me again. It had taken months for Rip and Nip to learn what refrigerators were for, but this skinny character had guessed right the first time.

I poured a bowl of milk and gave him a slice of leftover roast beef. He disposed of the beef in four bites and was noisily lapping the milk when Mom came down from upstairs, tying the sash of her faded red chenille bathrobe.

"What in the world?" she said. He looked up at her, his whiskers dripping milk, and turned on his flop-eared charm.

"Aww," Mom said. "Dave, come down here and see what we've got."

Dad came into the kitchen, putting on a wool shirt over his pajamas. As he sat down at the kitchen table and picked up his pipe, I explained what had happened to the beef.

"Oh, poor little thing," Mom said. "Look at him, he's still hungry. I'll make him a real supper." She took a pan of chicken broth from the Coldspot and warmed it on the stove. When it steamed, she poured it over a bowl of Gro-Pup and the stranger tore into the hot, wet kibbles, crunching and slobbering. The beagles whined from the dining room. They never got broth on their Gro-Pup.

"God, listen to him eat," Dad said. "It's like feeding time at the zoo. Don't give him any more, Charlotte—he'll founder."

"He was in the garage when I got home," I said. "I suppose somebody dumped him off."

"Probably," Dad said. Because our house in the woods was just outside the Manitowoc city limits, several times a year we had to find homes for dogs and cats that people abandoned to fend for themselves along the road.

The newcomer finished licking out his bowl, put his paws on Dad's knee, and wiped the last of the broth from his chin onto Dad's pajama leg.

"Well," Dad said, "we'll have to put a 'Found' ad in the paper for a couple of weeks and see if anybody calls. So don't go getting all attached to him."

"Yeah, right," Mom said, with a knowing smile. When it came to stray dogs, he was a bigger softy than she was; if it were solely up to him, we'd have a dozen.

"Anyway," she said, "if we do keep him, I've got an idea. We could call him Tuck. Listen to how it rolls off the tongue—Rip, Nip, and Tuck!"

Dad made a sour face. "I suppose. You're the clever one. But it sounds like a cheap law firm to me."

By this time it was past midnight. Dad opened the back door and let the dogs outside. "We should shut the new one in the kitchen tonight, just in case," he said. "He might not be housebroken."

About three o'clock I woke up and listened for whining or scratching from downstairs. The house was so quiet I began to wonder, so I went down for a look. Tuck was sleeping on his side under the kitchen table; he opened an eye and swished his tail back and forth on the linoleum.

"Good night, little guy," I said. Tuck replied with another swish. He had moved in.

It didn't take Tuck long to learn the ropes around our place. He answered to his name in two days, fit himself into the hierarchy below Rip and Nip, and became a retriever on his first tryout.

Some years earlier I had taught Nip to chase a ball and bring it back, but he was a hound by trade and fetched things strictly on a piecework basis; each retrieve had to be rewarded with an inch of hot dog. Tuck, on the other hand, played ball simply because he enjoyed it, or maybe because I enjoyed it. While the beagles slept on the lawn, I would hit a tennis ball to him with a softball bat, and he would field the ball and run to me with it, over and over.

As the days passed we lived in dread of a call from someone who would claim him. Fear clutched at our hearts every time the phone rang. Finally the two weeks were up and we canceled the ad in the

Manitowoc Herald-Times. After supper the next day, Dad slapped his thigh and Tuck jumped up into his lap.

"Well, young man, I guess you're ours now," he said. Tuck grinned, extended several inches of tongue, and licked Dad's face. We had been his from the start, of course.

Rip and Nip were purebred hunting dogs who expected a restful eight-month layoff between seasons. They were hidebound conservatives, set in their ways, and happy with their quiet, comfortable lives. Tuck was something altogether different, a radical with his own way of doing everything.

We discovered, for example, that unlike a lot of dogs Tuck lived in a world of three dimensions, up and down as well as back and forth. My bedroom was upstairs, and if I called the beagles from one of my windows, they would slowly awake from their daylong nap on the lawn and look around. If I called again they would sniff and whine and make short runs in search of me, north and south, east and west. They never thought of looking up.

But the first time I called Tuck from a bedroom window, he lifted his head, looked at me, and went to the back porch to be let in. As an experiment I blocked the back door open with a broom, went back up to my bedroom, and tossed a tennis ball to Tuck from my window.

He caught the ball on the first bounce, galloped to the back door, and then ran through the kitchen and up the stairs. He dropped the ball on the landing and went back down to the yard, where he looked up and waited for me to throw the ball again. From then on he was a confirmed up-looker.

Another of Tuck's peculiarities was his decision to ignore the milkman. Our milkman's name was Les, and he drove up in a big white van about five thirty in the morning, three days a week. As soon as the beagles heard the van's engine straining to climb our

steep driveway, they would jump from the beds they had been sleeping on and begin a hue and cry, thundering down the stairs and
through the house to the front door.

We had a standing order for milk on Monday, Wednesday, and
Friday, supplemented with orange juice and half-and-half on Monday and Friday. Les would open the door and put our bottles and
cartons inside while the dogs barked and wagged their tails.

"Hello, doggies," he would say, and then call out, "Anything else
today?" If Mom wanted whipping cream or butter she hollered her
order down the stairs. Sometimes Les left a pint of chocolate milk because he knew I liked it. He never charged us extra for chocolate milk.

On Tuck's first Wednesday and Friday with us he ran to the front
door with the beagles, just to see what was going on. But the following Monday he thought better of it. When the van pulled up the
driveway he jumped off my bed and put his paws on the windowsill
to watch Les come and go. Then he hopped back on the bed and
went to sleep again. I could almost hear the wheels going around in
his head:

The milkman does no harm.

No matter how much we bark, he always comes.

So why bother?

Tuck also upset the balance of power between the beagles and
the squirrels in our yard. We had a lot of big oak trees, and they
provided acorns and habitat for a couple of dozen gray squirrels.
Over the years the beagles and squirrels had worked out a kind of
entente; the dogs would disregard the squirrels if they kept their
distance, and most of the time they tolerated each other.

But every now and then a careless or overconfident squirrel would
wander too close, and there would be a brief and pointless chase. The
beagles would join forces and run after the squirrel, falling steadily
behind. The squirrel would climb the nearest oak, turn head-down,

and chatter. Within a few minutes the beagles would be asleep again and the squirrel would continue hunting acorns.

Tuck watched a few of these squirrel chases without joining in. He seemed to grasp that if the squirrels had a head start, dogs could not outrun them. So he introduced a new tactic: ambush.

Mom had planted a bed of day lilies in the lawn, and Tuck would lie hidden in it, his nose between his forepaws, waiting for a squirrel to get within a couple of feet. When one did, he would burst from concealment and run after it in great leaps, snapping at its whipping tail. He never caught any of the squirrels he chased, but he got close and he seemed pleased with that.

By midsummer, however, he tired of the squirrels and shifted his attention to our bantam chickens. We had eight hens and two roosters, and they lived in a wooden coop surrounded by a high fence in the backyard. On nice days we let them out to scratch in the yard and garden, and Tuck was fascinated with them.

Mom was washing the dishes one Saturday afternoon, occasionally checking on the chickens through the big kitchen window over the sink. Suddenly she took a second look. "Dave, come here," she said. "I think Tuck is after one of the chickens!"

Dad and I looked out the window. A hen had strayed close to the steep wooded ravine on the east side of our yard. Half-wild cats sometimes lurked in the ravine, preying on young songbirds and rabbits, and chickens too, if they had the chance. We suspected that cats had killed some of our hens in the past, but were never able to catch them in the act.

Tuck circled around the hen and got between it and the edge of the ravine. Then he trotted toward the hen; it turned and ran back to the flock, where there was safety in numbers.

"He's not trying to catch it, Charlotte, he's herding it," Dad said. "I wouldn't believe it if I hadn't seen it with my own eyes."

178

A couple of nights later, when the dogs were let out at bedtime, Tuck took off into the backyard at a dead run. In the faint light from the porch we saw him chasing something away from the chicken pen. We whistled up the beagles, but Tuck didn't come back with them. Dad and I sat up until midnight and finally Tuck appeared, strutting proudly but with some scratches on his muzzle and a bloody ear.

"This dog is too smart to tangle with a raccoon, and if he was after a skunk we'd know it," Dad said. "I'll bet he killed one of those stray cats, or gave it a hell of a scare, anyway."

From then on, Tuck had a mission in life. The chickens became his responsibility, and whenever we let them out of their pen, he guarded them and intervened if they wandered near the ravine or the big open field beyond the garden.

Then, one rainy night in early August, we let the dogs out and Tuck didn't come back. We waited up until midnight again, but this time there was no sign of him. The next morning, when Les put the milk inside the front door Mom called down to him.

"Pound of butter, Les," she said.

"OK," Les replied. "By the way, I brought your dog back."

"What?" Dad said. "Wait a minute!" He pulled on his pants and went downstairs. Les was standing just inside the front door, surrounded by the beagles. Tuck sat unconcernedly a couple of feet away.

"He was by the Wernicke farm the other side of 151, headed this way down the road," Les said. "I opened the door and he jumped right in."

"Well, I'll be damned," Dad said. "Thanks, Les."

"No trouble at all," Les said. "Here's your butter."

Tuck seemed happy to be back with us, but in mid-August he wandered off again. Three nights and days went by with no sign of him. After supper every night Mom, Dad, and I drove the back roads, looking for him. About eleven on the fourth night, Dad dropped Mom and me off at home but left the engine running.

"I'm not sleepy," he said. "I'm going to drive around a little more." Within an hour he was back, with Tuck riding in the front seat and looking out the window.

"You'll never guess where he was," Dad said. "He was at the floozy house."

The floozy house was the local name for a decaying farmstead five miles west of town. A woman of easy virtue lived there and was available at all hours.

"I pulled in the driveway to turn around," Dad said, "and in the headlights I could see Tuck sitting on her porch. I gave a whistle and he came running."

"Did she have any company?" Mom asked.

"She sure did," Dad said. He bent over and whispered to Mom.

"Dave, it couldn't be! Did you see him?"

"No, but who else around here drives a big black . . . ?" He whispered to Mom again and laughed. "It's always the psalm-singers who can't keep their pants on."

Tuck settled back in, but after a week he disappeared for the fourth time. The county fair was in progress, and the next day a policeman called. When he picked up the phone Dad could hear merry-go-round music in the background.

"Mr. Crehore, I've got your dog here at the fairgrounds," the policeman said. "I found him begging for bratwurst. If you come over and pick him up now I won't take him to the pound."

We jumped in the Studie and went to Tuck's rescue. He rode home on Mom's lap. "I wonder why he keeps running away," she said. "Is he looking for something, or what?"

"Beats me," Dad said. "I guess he's just a wanderer. Maybe it's the hound in him. Or maybe he ran off all the local cats and is hunting for more."

From then on we were careful to keep Tuck indoors at night, and he went back to his daytime routine, chasing the tennis ball, guarding the bantams, and wrestling gently with the beagles. But one night in September he slipped away and never came back.

We put a "Lost" ad in the newspaper and drove the highways and back roads for a week. This time we kept hoping for the phone to ring, but no one called. Tuck seemed to be gone for good. We mourned him for a month, imagining his wiry little body lying dead along the roadside. The beagles seemed to miss him too. A week or so before Thanksgiving Dad spoke up.

"We've got to quit moping around about Tuck," he said. "That dog is smart as a whip, and he's a survivor. He found us, and I'll bet you anything he's found himself another home by now."

That made us feel a little better, but I kept Tuck's tennis ball on the dresser in my bedroom. When I looked at it and remembered him smiling up at me, panting and waiting for me to throw it, I had trouble swallowing.

A year went by, then two. One day in the fall of 1961, Dad stopped at the camera store downtown and picked up a box of Kodachrome slides that had come back from the processing lab in Chicago. After supper Dad set up the projector and the screen in the living room, and we looked at the new slides he had taken. Then he pulled an older tray of slides from the cabinet by the fireplace and put it on the projector.

"Let's see what these are," he said. The first slide in the tray was of Tuck jumping high to catch a ball. None of us said anything, and after a few seconds Dad shut off the projector. The living room was pitch dark.

"What's the matter, Dave?" Mom asked.

"Nothing," he said. "But I guess this is as good a time as any to tell you—I know what happened to Tuck."

Dad took his pipe from his shirt pocket, filled it, and lit it. We could see his face in the light of the match as he drew the flame down into the tobacco.

"It was just dumb luck," he explained. "Last Sunday I was driving around south of Cato looking for places to hunt. I found a pretty good-looking rabbit swamp so I pulled in to the nearest farm to ask permission. And while I was talking to the farmer Tuck came out of the house with two little girls."

"I asked and the farmer said he just showed up one night in the fall of '59—it would have been a week or two after he left us. He was pretty ragged and the tags had come off his collar, the farmer said, so they patched him up and kept him."

"I almost claimed him then and there," Dad said, "but when I saw him playing ball with the little girls I just couldn't do it."

"Cato is ten miles away," Mom said. "Are you sure it was Tuck?"

"Positive," Dad replied. "The clincher was when the farmer said he'd had a lot of dogs, but this was the first one that herded chickens."

Mom turned on the lights, walked around behind Dad's chair, and rubbed his shoulders.

"I'm sorry," Dad said. "We all loved that little guy. But you asked me once why he kept running away. Well, maybe he was looking for a farm with two little girls to play with. Anyway, he's been there two years, so I guess his wandering days are over."

Mom smiled. "You made the right choice, Dave," she said. "You always make the right choice. That's why you married me!"

"You bet!" Dad exclaimed. He rolled up the screen and I put away the slides. But I've kept the memories handy.

Sweet and Sour Pie

The first Thanksgiving I can remember was in 1949, a year before Mom, Dad, and I moved to Wisconsin. It was the Thanksgiving when we had rabbit and french fries.

The entire Lorain, Ohio, branch of the Crehore family was there. Grandpa and Grandma, Mom and Dad, three aunts, three uncles, three cousins, and I gathered at Uncle Charlie and Aunt Betty's apartment that day, a grand total of twelve adults and four small boys. Aunt Betty, a home economics teacher, had volunteered to prepare the entire dinner, and its centerpiece was to be a twenty-pound turkey.

The day started early with a family Thanksgiving tradition—a mass rabbit hunt on the original Crehore homestead farm, led by Grandpa, with Dad and my four uncles serving as foot soldiers. They were supposed to hit the briar patches at 6:00 a.m. and be home by 11:00. Then they would clean up and arrive at Charlie and Betty's around noon, with wives and kids in tow.

The rabbit hunt was a success. The farm was a couple of miles away on the outskirts of town, and it was hunted only by relatives. That day, the six men collected a total of twenty cottontails, and they even got home on time.

But then the best-laid plans began to fall apart. First of all, it was harder than Betty had figured to fit twelve adults and four small boys around the table. Uncle George lived just around the corner, so he went home to fetch a card table and some extra chairs. But once that problem was solved, a bigger one surfaced. The bouquet of roasting turkey, which should have filled the apartment by then, was conspicuously absent. We sat shoulder to shoulder in the living room, and sniffed, and wondered.

Before long the truth came out. Betty opened the kitchen door about an inch and summoned her husband. "Charlie," she called, in a high-pitched and slightly quavering voice, "Charlie, would you come here, please?"

Charlie forced a nervous laugh and went into the kitchen, closing the door behind him. We could hear whispers. After about a minute he reappeared, his face as red as his hair. He smiled sheepishly.

"There will be a slight delay," he said. "The little woman forgot to light the oven."

It was at this point that I learned something about forbearance, and leadership, too. Grandpa and Grandma were the senior people present, so everyone turned to them for guidance. Grandma put a hand over her mouth, but her thin little shoulders were shaking and it was clear she was laughing. So was Grandpa. Finally he assumed a straight face and turned to Grandma.

"Such is life," he said. "A twenty-pound turkey will take about five hours, won't it, Anna?"

"At least," Grandma said. She pointed at me and my cousins. "The little fellas can't wait that long to eat," she said. "Why don't we fry up the rabbits—you said you had twenty of them, didn't you—and we could make potatoes, and there's a big colander of string beans at home, we could cook them up with some bacon. Run home and get the beans and the big cast-iron skillets and my boning knife and a pound of bacon and the oil."

"No sooner said than done," Grandpa said. "Boys, go get your rabbits."

We all lived within a mile or two of each other, so within a half hour the kitchen table was covered with cottontails, beans, bacon, and potatoes. Grandma put her arm around Aunt Betty to comfort her.

"Don't worry, Betty," Grandma said. "Everyone makes mistakes. Remember that root beer I made for the holidays last year, and every single bottle of it exploded on Christmas Eve? Well, that just goes to show you.

"Now," she continued, "let's make dinner. Dave and Charlie, fry up the bacon and boil the beans. Betty, slice the potatoes. George and Jack, take the rabbits outside and dress them. I'll fry them. Charlotte, could you make some biscuits?" And within about an hour and a half we were sitting down to rabbit and potatoes fried crisp in coconut oil, crunchy green beans with bacon, and biscuits full of melted butter.

Before I could stick a fork into my first piece of rabbit, Grandpa cleared his throat and stood up.

"It's customary to say a word of thanks before Thanksgiving dinner," he said, "and I am particularly thankful for two people—my wife and Franklin Delano Roosevelt, may God rest his soul. Amen."

"Amen!" we all repeated, and started to eat. The turkey, meanwhile, sat in the Frigidaire. Betty roasted it the next day, and the legend is that Charlie ate turkey sandwiches for seventeen consecutive days.

After we moved to Manitowoc in 1950, our Ohio relatives were five hundred miles away. That was a two-day drive in those days, so for our first six Manitowoc years, Thanksgiving dinner was shared only by our nuclear family and its two orbiting beagles. The beagles panted impatiently under the table while we ate, but after we finished our pie, we filled their bowls with dark meat and turkey skin. They ate ravenously and competitively, and it was a joy to watch them. Then they would lie distended on the back porch and be sick. But they didn't mind, because that gave them a chance to pick through everything, find the best stuff, and eat it again.

When I got into my teens, the new tradition was interrupted. In 1955, Mom and Dad joined a group of four couples, including a doctor and a dentist and their wives, who dined together about once a month. In the fall of 1957, when I turned fifteen, it was decided that the group would have Thanksgiving dinner at the home of the dentist. His wife would bake the pies and act as hostess, with the other couples bringing the turkey, potatoes, cranberries, and side dishes.

This division of labor was good in theory. The doctor's wife was a marvelous cook and so was Mom. But it failed in practice, because to protect our teeth the dentist's wife had baked green apple pies without sugar. They were inedible; even the women who daintily asked for "just a sliver" could not finish their slivers, and the dentist's wife was miffed.

But not as miffed as the doctor, who was nothing like the emaciated doctors so common today, doctors who run a marathon before breakfast. No, this doctor was an old-fashioned family M.D. who made house calls, and would give you a shot of penicillin right through the seat of your pajamas if you were shy about disrobing. This doctor lived for pie and had been saving room for it. He was known for his perfect frankness and inability to whisper, and when the dentist's wife overheard him using a medical term to describe the pie—"quinine," I believe it was—the atmosphere at the dentist's got distinctly chilly.

Besides the sour pie, there was another drawback to Thanksgiving at the dentist's: the nearness of Mary, who lived just around the corner and down the block.

Mary was the person for whom the term "nice girl" had been coined, and Mom was interested in getting us together. For weeks she prodded me into asking Mary out on a date Thanksgiving night. "It will be so convenient for both of you," Mom said, as though that mattered. Finally, one day after school I cornered Mary and summoned the nerve to ask her, and she accepted. It was to be my first unsupervised, unchaperoned date with an actual girl, and in the days leading up to Thanksgiving, I should have felt a pleasant anticipation.

But what I actually felt was dread and anxiety. For a first date, I would have preferred an ordinary girl who wouldn't expect much. Instead I had Mary, who was superior to me in every respect. At fifteen, she was good-looking, talented, a straight-A student, and a gifted athlete with an IQ of about 200. In addition to "nice girl," other terms that might have been invented to describe Mary were Phi Beta Kappa and summa cum laude. I had managed to get myself involved with another princess.

But a deal was a deal, and when Thanksgiving dinner was finally over, I walked leaden-footed to Mary's. She was ready and waiting, all smiles and wearing a fetching white duffle coat with a fur-trimmed hood. Standing on the porch with her before we started our long march downtown, I felt relieved about one thing: if nothing else, I stood about a half-inch taller than she, even with the fur trim.

The plan was to walk the three miles to the Mikadow Theater, take in a movie, go somewhere for a Coke afterward, and walk the three miles home. It was a few degrees above freezing, but as we walked along I found myself yawning and stumbling over my feet as we shuffled through the fallen leaves. I tried to suppress the yawns so Mary wouldn't think I was bored, but post-turkey lassitude had me in its thrall. And once I had flopped into a comfortable seat in the dark, overheated Mikadow, I was down for the count. Soon I was snoring, belching turkey and onion fumes, and, I strongly suspect, breaking wind as well—I can't say for sure, because I was asleep.

During the first reel, Mary poked me from time to time in an attempt to quiet me down, but after a while I guess she just gave up and waited for it to be over. We never saw much of each other after that, mostly because I was too embarrassed to face her. I distinctly remember a Friday night later that winter when I saw Mary coming my way down the sidewalk on Eighth Street. I crossed over in mid-block and pretended to look at a wristwatch in Rummele's window until she was out of sight.

From time to time I have wondered what might have happened if I had kept on seeing Mary—assuming, of course, that Mary would have kept on seeing me. Probably nothing; once you have exposed a nice girl to the full aftereffects of a heavy Thanksgiving dinner, a line has been crossed and things are never the same.

After 1960, I was in college, the navy, and then college again. My only Thanksgiving away from home was spent aboard a ship rolling her guts out in the Pacific. The motion of the ship slopped the yams into the cranberry sauce and sent the peas rolling into the ice cream, creating a mottled stew that we ate only because we were homesick. Except for those who were seasick—they ate nothing at all.

Thanksgiving started being fun again after I got married. My family ate sage and onion dressing, rutabagas, and mincemeat, apple, and pecan pie. My wife's relatives, on the other hand, were Germans and Norwegians who preferred bland and mild-mannered foods. My first Thanksgiving dinner at the in-laws was a shock; I found I had married into a family that stuffed the turkey with apples and raisins, ate dumplings instead of mashed potatoes, and regarded mincemeat pie with grave suspicion. There were compensations, though: Auntie Ruth's dumplings turned out to be chubby little poems, and my mother-in-law's apple pies weren't better than Mom's but in the ballpark.

The best part was that my wife's relatives ate Thanksgiving dinner at suppertime, while my parents, who had given up the society of the dentist, always served holiday meals at 1:00. So not only had I gained a wife, I had also gained a second Thanksgiving dinner.

Well, that was then. Today, the greatest generation of the Crehores and Lesters and Heckers and Sorensons is no longer with us, and those of us who were young in the 1950s have combined the family traditions. We have sage dressing and potato dumplings, mincemeat and apple pies, and pretty much eat all day and well into the evening.

Because, let's be honest. The best part of the whole Thanksgiving ritual is to slip into the kitchen about midnight, slice off some cold turkey, make a sandwich—heavy on the mayonnaise—warm up a dumpling and some dressing and gravy in the microwave, take a dollop of cranberry sauce out of the fridge, pour a glass of milk, and eat, preferably in the company of something good to read. If you still have room, a piece of apple pie with a little maple syrup on it will go down nicely.

And then you give thanks for the bounty, and for the people you love, who are sleeping quietly down the hall.

Envoi

I drove down to Manitowoc Rapids on a Saturday afternoon last January to have a look at the old schoolhouse. There have been a few changes.

For one thing, the Rapids State Graded building is now an Amvet post. Schools as small as Rapids used to be no longer exist. They have been replaced by big, consolidated places a long bus ride from home.

The mellow brick walls of Rapids school are still holding up, but the big windows that flooded our classrooms with sunlight have been removed and their frames filled in to save heat. A third-grader in Mrs. Eberhardt's room would find it hard to read *The Poky Little Puppy* by the light of the few panes of glass that remain. Still, I'm glad someone is using the place and taking care of it.

The sledding hill is paved now, and not as steep as it used to be.

There was a foot of snow on the ground in Rapids the day I was there, but there were no sled tracks, no snow forts or even footprints. No kids were visible anywhere. They were indoors watching television or fiddling with computers, I suppose. Their loss.

Geezers who return to the scenes of their youth always marvel at how small things look to them. But everything around Rapids State Graded looked about the same size to me, except for the lot across the street where we played the softball World Series. If anything, it seemed bigger. It has grown up in trees, some of them two feet in diameter, and the sewie ditch has been filled in, although there are still traces of it if you know where to look. The lot is now officially a park, and a sign states the rules: "Mini Park No Dogs No Baseball."

No dogs? In the early '50s, the neighborhood dogs played with us at recess and set their internal clocks by our lunch hour. In good weather we took our lunchboxes outside and the dogs would gather around and wait for scraps while we drank milk from our thermoses and ate our bologna sandwiches. Now there are no kids and no lunchboxes and nothing to attract a dog in the first place.

Before I left I tried to estimate the length of Doyle's home run. It was 250 feet, I figured, or maybe more—a prodigious distance for a fourteen-year-old boy to hit a wet softball.

I was hungry for some penny candy, but Felix's store was gone. The building was still there, though. It's a doctor's office now.

The taverns on the corner have been replaced, one by a bank and the other by a convenience store, one of those magical places that can turn a twenty-dollar bill into three gallons of gas and a pack of cigarettes. I pulled in and filled the tank in my truck. Watching the numbers flicker on the pump, I calculated it would take almost $7.50 worth of gas to make the round-trip from Green Bay to Manitowoc Rapids. In 1950, seven bucks would have bought twenty-six gallons, enough to drive to Ohio for Christmas.

I was still hungry for something sweet, so I went into the store and looked around. There were shelves and shelves of candy, forty or fifty varieties, but all of it the same old stuff, sealed in people-proof wrappers that have to be hacked open with a mumblety-peg knife. I saw no candy in big glass jars and, God knows, nothing for a penny.

As I drove home I wondered how to wrap up the '50s.

What a sweet and sour decade it had been: The Korean War and McCarthy. Nixon and Checkers and Pat's "respectable Republican cloth coat." A missile gap and "duck and cover" and fallout shelters. We had cars with tail fins and Firedome engines and a powerful thirst for gasoline. We had Rosa Parks in the back of the bus and Emmett Till on the bottom of the Tallahatchie River.

But we also had the Milwaukee Braves and Henry Aaron, Elvis Presley and Miles Davis, James Dean and Ozzie Nelson, Jack Kerouac and Dave Brubeck, and Billy Graham. We had factories that made televisions and coffee pots and shoes. It seemed like everybody had a good job, and a house with a 4 percent mortgage, and a union card that meant something. We never locked our doors. We had won the war and we believed in ourselves. We had cold winters and cool summers and good fishing. And every August, the county fair.

Maybe it was the best of times.

Enso?

Glossary

A&P. Short for the Great Atlantic & Pacific Tea Company, A&P was founded in 1859 and was once America's largest food retailer, with 14,000 stores nationwide in 1930. Today, it has shrunk to 456 stores concentrated on the eastern seaboard. In Manitowoc the A&P was on Washington Street in the vicinity of the Mikadow Theater and a tavern called, quite innocently in those days, the Gay Bar.

Big Chip. A nickname for the Chippewa Flowage, located in northwest Wisconsin near the city of Hayward. Formed by the damming of the Chippewa and Chief rivers in 1923, it is Wisconsin's third-largest lake and covers 15,300 acres or about 24 square miles. A labyrinth of peninsulas, bays, islands, and floating bogs, it can be hard to navigate but affords excellent fishing and wildlife viewing.

car ferry. Car ferries were large steel ships that crossed Lake Michigan between Wisconsin and Michigan. Primarily, they carried railroad cars around the Chicago bottleneck, but they also carried automobiles and passengers. One ferry, the S. S. Badger, still sails out of Manitowoc, but it no longer carries railroad cars.

CCC. The Civilian Conservation Corps was one of the most popular and effective New Deal programs enacted to fight the effects of the Great Depression. From 1933 to about 1941, the CCC provided work, lodging, and food for hundreds of thousands of unemployed young men. They did forestry work, planted trees, worked in national, state, and local parks, and constructed many miles of roads and trails. The program was estimated to cost $1,000 per man per year. "CCC boys" were paid $30 a month, of which $25 had to be sent home.

Checkers speech. On September 23, 1952, Richard M. Nixon, the Republican candidate for vice president, made one of the first political speeches to be televised nationally. He had been accused of accepting $16,000 (some said $18,000) in illegal campaign contributions; Democrats and some Republicans called for him to leave the ticket. Nixon used the speech to rebut the charges, calling the accusations a smear and claiming that he had spent the money not for personal needs but for office and travel expenses. In the speech, Nixon threw mud at his political opponents and summarized an audit of his personal finances, which showed modest assets and liabilities. He denied the assertion that his wife, Pat, had a fur coat, claiming that she wore a "respectable Republican cloth coat."

Nixon did, however, admit to accepting one personal gift, a black-and-white cocker spaniel, which his little girls named Checkers. In the most memorable lines of the speech, Nixon said his girls loved the dog and that he was going to keep it, no matter what. No one, of course, had ever suggested that the Nixons should return the dog, but the use of Checkers as a "straw dog" worked and Nixon stayed on the ticket.

cigarette machine. Now almost extinct, cigarette machines were once a fixture of every bar, restaurant, lunch counter, and bus station. Customers in the early '50s would insert a quarter, or at the most 35 cents, pull a knob, and receive a pack. Knowledgeable smokers confined their choices to the most popular brands—Camel, Lucky Strike, Pall Mall,

Philip Morris, Old Gold, and Chesterfield—because they were the most likely to be fresh. Slower-selling brands like Fatima, Kool, and Herbert Tareyton sometimes dried out in the machine.

DeSoto. The DeSoto was a medium-priced, moderately successful automobile sold by Chrysler from 1929 until 1961. For some reason, it was named after the early Spanish explorer Hernando DeSoto. During its first years, the DeSoto was an upright and boxy car, but in the late 1930s it was given low-slung, streamlined styling. The DeSoto may have been doomed from the outset because it had to compete with its Chrysler stablemate Dodge, as well as Studebaker, Willys-Knight, and various General Motors cars. The 1961 DeSoto was pathetically ugly, with tail fins, four headlights in a slanted configuration, and two grilles, one above the other.

Door County. The peninsular "thumb" of northeast Wisconsin, extending into Lake Michigan. Once a bucolic place of cherry orchards, small farms, cozy clapboard villages, and commercial fishermen, it has been extensively citified and commercialized by upscale tourists, retired people, and the canny locals who cater to them. Its scenic beauty, most of it preserved within five state parks, is still worth a look. But pack a lunch; Door County is widely known as the home of the nine-dollar hamburger.

enso. A northeast Wisconsin word that means "Isn't it so?" Pronounced en-SO, with a rising inflection at the end.

fedora. A soft wool felt men's hat, popular from the late 1800s through about 1960. A fedora had a brim of varying width, a lengthwise crease down the center of the crown, and dual pinches in front. You can see fedoras in action on the heads of such classic film heroes as Humphrey Bogart (*The Maltese Falcon*), Clark Gable (*It Happened One Night*), Spencer Tracy (*Bad Day at Black Rock*), and Jimmy Stewart (*Vertigo*).

Fabled Green Bay Packers coach Vince Lombardi was one of the last public figures to wear a fedora.

flat tire. Almost a thing of the past today, "flats" were a common occurrence from the earliest days of motoring until well into the 1960s. Tires in those days were not belted with steel, so it was easy for a nail, a shard of broken glass, or even a sharp stone to penetrate a tire's tread and soft inner tube. While most flats were caused by slow leaks, some were sudden, explosive, and scary, particularly at highway speed. In addition to a full-sized spare tire, prudent motorists carried a jack, a lug wrench, a tube repair kit, a tire pump, and a tire iron at all times.

If you got a flat and didn't have a spare, you had to jack up the appropriate corner of the car, loosen the lug nuts, remove the wheel and tire, use the tire iron to peel the tire off the wheel, pull the inner tube out of the tire casing, find the hole in the tube, and glue a patch over it. When the glue dried, you put the inner tube back into the tire, used the tire iron to put the tire back on the wheel, inflated the tube with the pump, retightened the lug nuts, and let the car down off the jack.

Ford, Model A. The Model A Ford, produced from 1927 until 1931, replaced the venerable Model T. Almost five million Model A Fords were built. The car sold for $500, had a four-cylinder, 3.3-liter engine that developed 40 horsepower, got 20–30 miles per gallon, and could attain a speed of 65 miles per hour.

Ford, Model T. The Model T Ford was the first affordable American automobile, "the car that put America on wheels." It was also known as the Tin Lizzie and the Flivver. With its rugged construction and high ground clearance, the T was ideally suited to American roads; outside cities, most roads at the time were paved with gravel, mud, or snow. About fifteen million Model Ts were built between 1908 and 1927. The car had a four-cylinder, 2.9-liter engine that developed 20 horsepower, got 20 miles per gallon, and could be driven—cautiously—at speeds up to 45 miles per hour. Because the Model T had no fuel pump and depended on gravity to move gasoline from its tank to the carburetor, it could not go up steep hills in forward gear and had to climb them in reverse. The first Model Ts cost $850, but by 1920, mass production and economies of scale brought the price down to $300.

Frau. German for "Mrs."

Gardner, Ava (1922–90). Back in the '50s, when a man or boy got a new wallet for Christmas it usually came with a picture of a beautiful movie star inside, behind a little celluloid window. Ava Gardner was one of those stars. From a poor and rural background in North Carolina, Ava was "discovered" in 1941 and signed a contract with MGM. She appeared in about sixty films and was nominated for an Oscar. A brunette with green eyes and a spectacular figure, she overwhelmed men with smoldering half smiles; she could appear powerful and dominating one minute and vulnerable the next. She was married three times, to Mickey Rooney and bandleader Artie Shaw for about a year apiece and to Frank Sinatra for six years.

Holstein. The familiar black-and-white dairy cow, the Holstein was first brought to North America from the Netherlands in the 1850s. A mature Holstein weighs about fifteen hundred pounds and can produce two thousand gallons of milk per year.

Howdy Doody. OK, kids, let's all sing "It's Howdy Doody Time," to the tune of "Ta-ra-ra Boom-de-ay"! *Howdy Doody* was an inane but immensely popular children's show that aired on NBC-TV from 1947 until 1960. Howdy was a marionette whose voice was provided by the show's host, Buffalo Bob, who dressed up as a cowboy. In addition to his scratchy, un-kid-like voice, Howdy had another problem—he couldn't hold still. No matter what he was doing or saying, Howdy was in constant motion, tap dancing, shuffling, and waving his hands and arms in fluttering gestures.

Other marionette characters included Howdy's sister Heidi Doody (clever, enso?), Mayor Phineas T. Bluster, and Princess Summerfall Winterspring. Besides Buffalo Bob, the principal human character of the show was Clarabell, a mute clown who communicated with horns and seltzer bottles like Harpo Marx. I always felt that kids who really enjoyed *Howdy Doody* were short on self-esteem.

Hudson. Hudson automobiles were built in Detroit from 1909 until 1954. They were reasonably priced and innovative, slightly upscale from the more numerous Fords and Chevrolets. For a time, Hudson also produced the Essex and Terraplane cars. Hudsons were among the first cars to feature dual brakes, oil pressure gauges and ammeters, automatic transmissions, and independent front suspension. With their strong, light bodies and high-compression engines, Hudson "Hornets" were NASCAR champions from 1951 through 1954. Hudson merged with Nash-Kelvinator in 1954 to form American Motors Corporation in Kenosha, Wisconsin.

latakia. A black and pungent pipe tobacco grown in Syria and Cyprus, latakia is cured and seasoned with the smoke from burning pine, cedar, and various herbs. Despite its menacing appearance and heavy aroma, latakia is mild to smoke and low in nicotine. It is a principal ingredient of what are called English or Scottish pipe tobacco mixtures. A little latakia goes a long way.

Lombardo, Guy (1902–77). A Canadian bandleader who fronted a group known as the Royal Canadians. Famous for "the sweetest music this side of heaven," Lombardo's band featured saccharine saxophones playing sentimental dance tunes and "businessman's bounce." It had one of the longest-running gigs imaginable, doing a live New Year's Eve broadcast from the Roosevelt Hotel in New York for thirty years, 1929–59, and playing "Auld Lang Syne" at midnight.

Lorain, Ohio. A middle-sized shipbuilding and steel mill town on the Lake Erie shore about twenty-five miles west of Cleveland. Compared to Manitowoc in the '50s, which ran mainly to Germans, Lorain was a bubbling racial and cultural stew of Yankee pioneers, blacks, Puerto Ricans, Poles, and Hungarians. The steel mill produced powerful air pollutants and supplied them to all, regardless of creed or color. Lorain had air with real character—air you could see.

MacArthur, General Douglas (1880–1964). A lifelong U.S. Army officer, MacArthur was much loved and much hated. His résumé is far too extensive to go into here; suffice it to say that in the early days of World War II, the U.S. and Philippine forces he commanded were driven back by the Japanese to the Bataan peninsula and the small fortress island of Corregidor in Manila Bay. Under orders from Washington, MacArthur, with his family and aides, escaped from the island in a PT boat and left the trapped soldiers and sailors behind to be captured by the Japanese. Arriving in Australia, he proclaimed, "I came through and I shall return." The fact that he said "I" rather than "we" is an insight into his character; his military skill was exceeded only by his grandiosity and showmanship. Eventually, as commander of allied forces in the southwest Pacific, he did return and reconquer the Philippines.

When the war ended, MacArthur became commander of the U.S. occupation of Japan, and then was put in charge of U.S. and U.N. forces in the first year of the Korean War. Disobeying orders, MacArthur called for war with China and in 1951 was dismissed by President Harry S. Truman. In a final address to Congress, MacArthur made the second of his two most famous statements: "Old soldiers never die; they just fade away." There was talk of his running for president, but nothing came of it.

McCarthy, Senator Joseph Raymond. Wisconsin has little to be ashamed of, other than the fact that its citizens repeatedly elected Joe McCarthy, first as a judge and then as a U.S. senator. It is impossible for anyone of any political stripe to be objective about McCarthy, so I won't even try.

McCarthy, a native of Grand Chute near Appleton, Wisconsin, was a scheming, lying, dipso demagogue who led a reign of terror in the 1950s, claiming to know of hundreds of "commanists" in government, precious few of whom were ever discovered or named. He was abetted by the Washington press of the time, which printed his wild speculations and slanders without asking any of the obvious questions.

Because he was a circuit judge, McCarthy received an automatic commission as a second lieutenant after he volunteered for the Marine Corps in 1942, although he later claimed to have enlisted as a "buck private." He served as an intelligence officer with a dive-bomber squadron in the South Pacific and flew twelve combat missions as a gunner-observer in the backseat of a dive-bomber. He used a picture of himself in a flying helmet and goggles in his campaign literature, dubbing himself "Tail-Gunner Joe." After the war he claimed to have flown thirty-two missions, enough to qualify him for the Distinguished Flying Cross, which was awarded to him in 1952. Eventually his excesses caught up with him; he was censured by the Senate in 1954 and died of acute hepatitis in 1957.

In the 1990s I attended a series of watershed planning meetings in the Outagamie County Courthouse in Appleton. Entering the building for the first time, I was astounded to find a bust of Tail-Gunner Joe on a pedestal in the vestibule. From then on I brought a paper grocery bag from home and placed it over the bust on my way into the courthouse. The bags were always removed by the time I left a couple of hours later. I understand that the bust is now in a museum.

magazine plug. A wooden or plastic stick that is inserted into the tubular magazine of a pump or semiautomatic shotgun to reduce the total capacity of the gun to three rounds. Required by law for the hunting of migratory birds and waterfowl.

Manitowoc. In the 1950s, a manufacturing and shipbuilding city of about 25,000 on the Wisconsin shore of Lake Michigan, ninety miles north of Milwaukee. Was and is one of the neatest, most "kept-up," and well-governed communities to be found anywhere, with an excellent school and park system. During World War II, the Manitowoc shipyard produced twenty-eight submarines. Pronounced MAN-a-ta-walk.

Mein Kampf. Adolph Hitler was charged with treason after the Beer Hall Putsch, his abortive attempt to overthrow the German government in 1923. He was sentenced to five years of imprisonment, of which he served about a year. During his time in prison he wrote *Mein Kampf* (*My Struggle*), a book that outlined his past, his view of the world, and his plans for the future. It was all there: the racism and anti-Semitism, the notion of German destiny leading to domination of the world, and a lot of nonsense about the "Aryan" master race. If world leaders had read the book in the 1930s, when Hitler was rising to power in Germany, a lot of death and destruction might have been avoided.

Mikadow. See **WOMT.**

mumblety-peg. A game of skill and luck played with pocketknives, mumblety-peg has hundreds of variations. A basic version involved tossing a pocketknife gently a foot or two into the air and hoping the blade would stick into the ground when it landed. Then the player would try to make the knife rotate twice in the air before landing blade-first, then three times, and so forth.

New Deal. A system of federal programs, statutes, and regulations that saved capitalism from itself during the Great Depression of the 1930s.

P-51. Nicknamed the Mustang, the P-51 was World War II's most successful Allied fighter plane. In the opinion of many, it was also the best looking and best sounding. Mustangs were built by North American Aviation and powered by 12-cylinder, 2,000-horsepower supercharged Rolls-Royce Merlin engines manufactured in the United States by the

Packard Motor Car Company. Advanced versions of the Mustang could fly to forty thousand feet and attain speeds of over four hundred miles per hour with the throttle at "war emergency." Mustangs were designed to escort American bombers such as the B-17 on daylight raids over Germany, and at the time were the only fighters with enough range to go there and back. They were also used, with resounding success, for fighter sweeps and ground attack. The P-47 Thunderbolt, or "Jug," was in the same league as the Mustang but lacked its panache. Civilian-owned Mustangs are still flying as "warbirds" in air shows.

Pflueger Supreme. A fishing reel of the type called bait-casting, the original Supreme was made in the United States and featured a transverse spool for the line. It was mounted on the top of the rod grip and controlled by the thumb. Failure to thumb it correctly created backlashes of tangled line that could take minutes or hours to pick out. These backlashes would occur only when the fish were biting.

popple. A familiar Wisconsin name for trees of two species: the quaking aspen, *populus tremuloides,* and the large-toothed aspen, *populus grandidentata.* Popples are fast growing and short lived, and their wood is used primarily in the manufacture of paper.

record, 78-rpm. The 78s were large, thick platters with a playing time of only a few minutes per side. Such recordings of classical works came in cardboard boxes called albums, with paper sleeves for as many as ten records. An album containing enough 78s for a long work, such as a Gustav Mahler symphony, would weigh several pounds. Liner notes that analyzed the music were pasted inside the albums, and local radio announcers with time to fill sometimes read them over the air, joyfully mispronouncing the Italian, French, and German words.

respectable Republican cloth coat. See **Checkers speech.**

sheepshead. Of European origin, sheepshead (*Schafkopf* in German) is a complex card game for two to eight people using a thirty-two-card deck. I never learned to play sheepshead, but I watched many games. There was always a lot of shouting, punctuated by the slamming down of cards. Sometimes beer was involved.

Studebaker. The Studebaker Corporation, of South Bend, Indiana, was founded in 1852 and originally built wooden wagons, including the fabled Conestoga. Studebaker got into the car business with the Studebaker Electric in 1897 and built its first gasoline-powered automobiles in 1913. After various mergers and receiverships, Studebaker went out of the automobile business in 1966.

Our family owned Studebakers for more than twenty years, starting with a 1939 two-door, two-seat business coupe that Mom bought new for $660 and drove throughout the war years. After the war, we owned a Champion convertible, a Commander, and three station wagons. "Studies" were economical, reasonably sturdy cars with a feature called the Hill-Holder that was prized in cities like Duluth and San Francisco. If you had to stop for a traffic light while going up a hill, you would depress the clutch and step firmly on the brake. Then, wonder of wonders, you could take your foot off the brake pedal, and the brakes would be locked on by the Hill-Holder. When the light changed, you fed a little gas and eased up the clutch pedal, and as soon as the clutch began to engage, the Hill-Holder released the brake, enabling you to make a smooth start on an upgrade without rolling backward. Sheer genius.

Two Rivers. A small Wisconsin city on the Lake Michigan shore, about seven miles north of Manitowoc. Known locally as TR or Carptown (and sometimes pronounced T'rivers), Two Rivers is believed to be the original home of the ice-cream sundae. In 1881, a customer asked Edward C. Berner, the owner of a Two Rivers ice-cream parlor, to scoop up some vanilla and put chocolate syrup on it. Selling for five cents, sundaes soon came in a variety of flavors, including apple cider. The name "sundae" may stem from the fact that at first the concoctions were sold only on Sundays.

wall-hanger. A shotgun that is too old or unsafe to be fired, and is hung on the wall to create an outdoorsy atmosphere. A wall-hanger may also be converted into a floor lamp, with light bulbs protruding from its muzzles. Not to be confused with a "closet queen," a shotgun that is too expensive, rare, and beautiful to be fired or even handled very much.

Waring, Fred (1900–1984). Fred Waring was the proficient and popular leader of the Pennsylvanians, a choral ensemble heard on radio, recordings, and TV for many years. Known as "Mr. Waring" and never as "Fred," Waring was a skilled conductor and composer. He was also the financial backer of an electric mixer called the "Waring Blendor," well known to Daiquiri drinkers everywhere.

WOMT. Manitowoc's local radio station, owned by Francis Kadow, a neighbor of ours when we moved into town in the '60s. He also owned the Mikadow Theater, named after himself with an allusion, perhaps, to the Gilbert and Sullivan operetta. WOMT's call letters were an acronym for Wisconsin's Only Mikadow Theater, but Manitowoc kids believed the initials stood for Women Open Men's Trousers.

Zippo. A masterpiece of American technology and business sense, the Zippo windproof lighter was first manufactured in Bradford, Pennsylvania, in 1932. It sold for $1.98 and featured sturdy construction, reliable functioning, one-handed operation, and a lifetime warranty. Since then about 400 million Zippos have been sold, they are still made in Bradford, and the warranty still applies. Zippos have a hinged metal cap that is held closed by a spring and toggle. When the lighter is opened for use, this mechanism makes a distinctive metallic click that is unmistakably the sound of a Zippo. I still have and use a Zippo purchased by my grandfather in 1936. The cap hinge is getting a little wobbly, and one of these years I may send it in for a free repair. I suspect it will be lighting long after my fire has gone out.